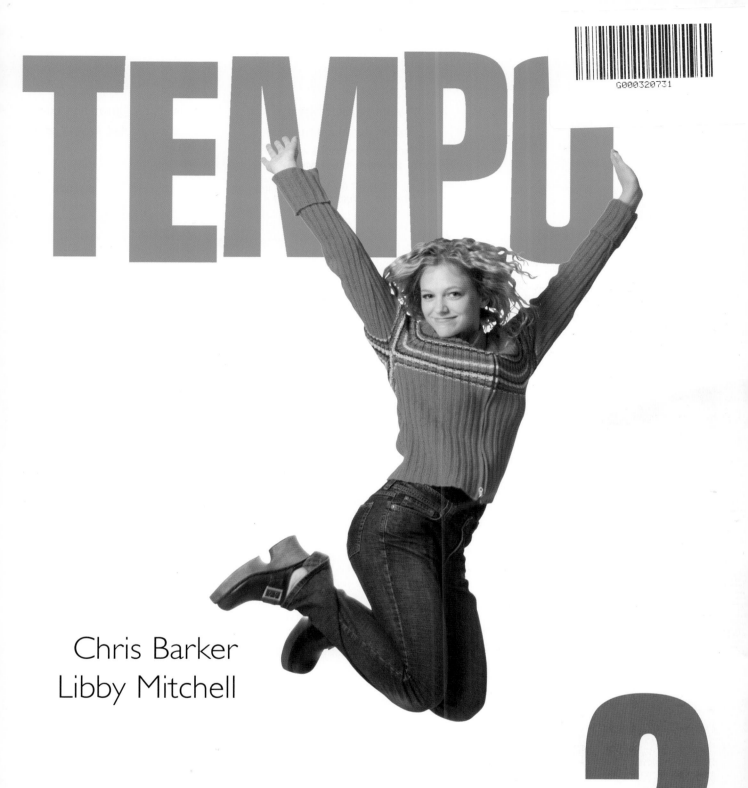

TEMPO

Chris Barker
Libby Mitchell

Student's Book 3

MACMILLAN

1

1   **Listen and read.**

Hi!

Hi, I'm Eddie. It's short for Edward.

Hello. My name's Adam.

I'm 14. I come from Cambridge, in England.
I haven't got any brothers and sisters – I'm an
only child. I go to Parkside School. My favourite
subjects are History and English.
I like football. I play for Cambridge Juniors. In my
free time I like reading and listening to music.

Hello. My name's Rachel.

And my name's Becky.
It's short for Rebecca.

We're from Cambridge in England.
We play for Cambridge Juniors.
And right now we're in Italy. We're playing
in the Junior Club Cup.

Name	Adam Walker	Rebecca (Becky) Grant	Edward (Eddie) Green	Rachel Andrews
Age	14	14	14	14
Hometown	Cambridge	Cambridge	Barton, near Cambridge	Ely, near Cambridge
Family	no brothers or sisters	a sister	a brother, two sisters	a brother
School	Parkside School	Parkside School	Comberton Village College	King's School, Ely
Favourite subjects	English, History	Art, P.E. (sports)	Science, Design and Technology	Maths, Spanish
Sports	football	football, volleyball	football, rugby	football, swimming
Free time	reading, listening to music	going out with friends	quad biking, cooking	shopping, going to the cinema

Read and speak

2) **Read the information about each person. Work with a partner. Imagine you are Becky, Eddie or Rachel.**

A Hello. My name's Becky/Eddie. I'm 14 …

Write

3) **Now write about yourself. Use Adam's text as a model.**

My name's Isabella/Luca. I'm 13. I'm from …

Module 1

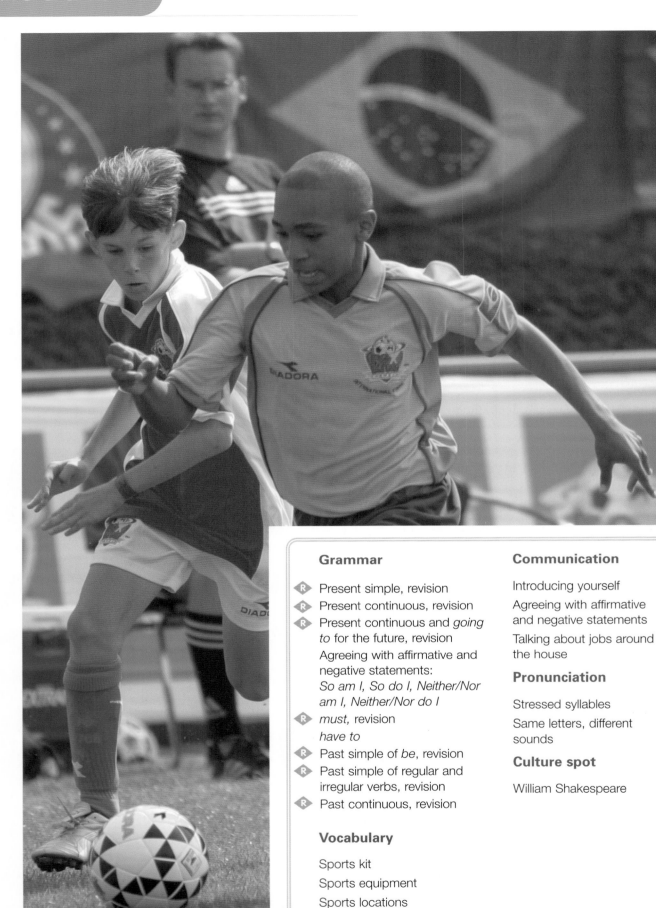

Grammar

- R Present simple, revision
- R Present continuous, revision
- R Present continuous and *going to* for the future, revision

  Agreeing with affirmative and negative statements:
  So am I, So do I, Neither/Nor am I, Neither/Nor do I
- R *must,* revision

  have to
- R Past simple of *be*, revision
- R Past simple of regular and irregular verbs, revision
- R Past continuous, revision

Vocabulary

Sports kit
Sports equipment
Sports locations
Transport

Communication

Introducing yourself
Agreeing with affirmative and negative statements
Talking about jobs around the house

Pronunciation

Stressed syllables
Same letters, different sounds

Culture spot

William Shakespeare

1

Sports kit

 1 football boots

 2 trainers

 3 shorts

 **4** tracksuit

 5 swimming trunks

 6 swimming costume

 7 swimming goggles

 **8** football/rugby shirt

 **9** T-shirt

 10 tennis skirt

Sports equipment

11 ball **12** racket **13** bat **14** club

Sports locations

15 football/rugby pitch
16 baseball field
17 basketball/volleyball court
18 tennis court
19 swimming pool
20 athletics track
21 race track
22 golf course
23 racecourse
24 gym

Pronunciation

Stressed syllables

2 Listen and underline the stressed syllables in these words and phrases.

1	<u>swi</u>mming	<u>swi</u>mming pool
2	football	football pitch
3	rugby	rugby shirt
4	tennis	tennis skirt
5	basketball	basketball court
6	athletics	athletics track
7	gymnastics	

1a Write the equipment and/or location for each sport.

1 football .ball, football pitch.
2 basketball
3 baseball
4 golf
5 tennis
6 swimming
7 athletics
8 gymnastics
9 horse racing
10 motor racing

3 Choose a sport. Say what you wear.

A When I play tennis I wear a tennis shirt, shorts and trainers.

B When I do gymnastics I wear ...

C When I go swimming I wear ...

1b Now listen and check.

Remember!
play football, rugby, baseball, basketball, volleyball, golf, tennis
do athletics, gymnastics
go swimming

The match starts at 11

- Present simple, revision
- Present continuous, revision
- Present continuous and *going to* for the future, revision
- Introducing yourself
- Agreeing with affirmative and negative statements: *So am I, So do I, Neither/Nor am I, Neither/Nor do I*

Listen and read

1 Listen and read.

Eddie	Sorry I'm late.
Becky	You're always late.
Eddie	No, I'm not.
Rachel	Eddie, this is Tommaso. He plays for Italy.
Eddie	Ciao, Tommaso. Does our match start at 11?
Tommaso	Yes, it does.
Rachel	Do you want some orange juice, Eddie?
Eddie	Yes, please ... and some cereal, and a banana, and some bread, and ...
Becky	Eddie!
Eddie	I always eat a good breakfast before a match.

Comprehension

2 **Choose the correct answer to each question.**

No, he isn't.	No, it doesn't.
~~Yes, he is.~~	Yes, she does.
No, he doesn't.	Yes, he does.

1 Is Eddie late? ...Yes, he is....
2 Is Tommaso English?
3 Does Rachel know Tommaso?
4 Does Eddie know Tommaso?
5 Does the boys' match start at 10 o'clock?
6 Does Eddie like a big breakfast?

Grammar focus

(R) The Present simple of be

Affirmative

I am (I'm)
You are (You're)
He is/She is/It is (He's/She's/It's) } late.
We are (We're)
You are (You're)
They are (They're)

How do you form the negative of be, Present simple?

How do you form questions?

How many examples of the verb be can you find in the dialogue?

Grammar practice

(3) Complete the sentences.

Affirmative

1 Sorry we **'re** .... late.
2 This .... my friend, Tommaso.
3 I .... Italian.
4 You .... English.
5 They .... from Cambridge.

Negative

6 The match **isn't** .... at 10 o'clock.
7 Wait for me! I .... ready.
8 Those .... my trainers. They're Patrick's.
9 We .... from London. We're from Cambridge.
10 Don't laugh! It .... funny!

Questions

11 ... **Are** ...... you ready?
12 .... English your favourite subject?
13 .... I late?
14 .... Emily your sister?
15 .... they here on holiday?

Listen

(4) Listen to two other members of the Cambridge Junior team. Complete the chart.

Name	Matthew	Kristy
Age		
Hometown	Cambridge	Cambridge
Family		
School	Parkside School	St Mary's
Favourite subjects		
Sports and free time activities		

Grammar focus

(R) Present simple

Affirmative

I/You/We/They play (football).
He/She/It plays (football).

How many examples of the Present simple can you find in the dialogue in Exercise 1?

Speak

(5) Work with a partner. Partner A: Tell your partner about Matthew. Partner B: Tell your partner about Kristy.

A Matthew is 13. He lives in Cambridge ...

B Kristy is 14. She lives in Cambridge ...

(6) Write an interview with Matthew or Kristy.

You   Hello. What's your name?
Mathew   My name's ....

1

Listen and read

7 **Listen and read.**

Becky	Where's Tommaso?
Rachel	He's there, look. He's wearing the number 8 shirt. He's playing really well.
Becky	Adam and Eddie aren't playing very well. Come on, Eddie, you aren't running! No wonder after all that breakfast!
Rachel	He's doing his best. Don't be horrible!

Becky	Look! Eddie's in front of the goal!
Rachel	Yes! It's a goal. Well done, Eddie!
Becky	It's half-time. One-nil. We're winning!

Comprehension

8 **Answer the questions.**

1 Who's wearing number 8?
   ..Tommaso..

2 Who's playing really well?

3 At the start of the match, which team isn't playing very well, the English team or the Italian team?

4 Who isn't running?

5 Who's winning at half-time?

Grammar focus

Present continuous

Affirmative

I'm playing football (at the moment).

You're playing

He's/She's/It's playing

We're/You're/They're playing

Do you remember how to form the negative and questions in the Present continuous?

How many examples of the Present continuous can you find in the dialogue?

Grammar practice

9a **Complete the sentences using the verbs in the box in the Present continuous.**

play	wear	not run
not play	win	~~watch~~

1 Rachel and Becky ..are watching... the match.

2 Tommaso .... the number 8 shirt.

3 Becky says, 'Eddie, you .... !'

4 Adam and Eddie .... for the English team.

5 At first Adam and Eddie .... very well.

6 At half-time Becky says, 'We ....!'

9b **Write questions and answers using the Present continuous.**

1 (you/feel) OK, Eddie? ✗/I

.Are you feeling OK, Eddie?....

.No, I'm not.................................

2 (we/win) ? ✓/we

3 (Tommaso/run) towards the goal? ✓/he

4 (Rachel and Becky/help) Eddie to the side of the pitch? ✗/they

5 (you/watch) the match, Rachel? ✓/I

🎧 Listen and read

10 **Listen and read. Put the photos in the correct order.**

Rachel	They're coming back onto the pitch.
Becky	Come on boys!
Rachel	What's the matter? Why is Eddie holding his ankle?
Becky	Oh, no. He's coming off the pitch.
Rachel	Adam and James are helping him.
Rachel	Are you feeling OK, Eddie?
Eddie	Yes, I'm OK.
Eddie	What's happening?
Becky	Tommaso's got the ball. He's running towards the goal.
Rachel	It's a goal!
Announcement	Final score: Italy 1 – England 1.

Speak

11 **Work with a partner. Point to a photo and ask your partner: What's happening in this photo? Use the verbs in the box to ask and answer.**

help	talk (to)	kick the ball
hold	run (towards)	come back
watch	come off	

A What's Rachel doing in this picture?

B She's talking to Eddie.

A What are Adam and James doing in this picture?

a b c d e 1

7

 Listen and read

12 **Listen and read.**

Rachel	Well played!
Tommaso	Thanks! Are you playing later?
Rachel	Yes, I am.
Becky	So am I. It's our last game.
Tommaso	Good luck!
Rachel	Thanks. Are you going to the disco this evening?
Tommaso	Yes, see you there. Bye!

Rachel	I think Tommaso is really nice.
Becky	So do I.
Eddie	So do I!
Becky	Shut up, Eddie! You're just jealous!
Rachel	What are you going to do this afternoon?
Eddie	I'm going to work out at the gym. I'm going to have muscles like Tommaso's!
Adam	He's joking. We're going to watch your match, of course. And then we're going to get ready for the disco.

Comprehension

13 **Answer the questions.**

1 When is the girls' match? ....It's this afternoon...
2 What's special about their match?
3 When is the disco?
4 What do Rachel and Becky think of Tommaso?
5 Is Eddie serious about going to the gym?

Grammar practice

14 **Look at the grammar focus box. Then agree with these statements.**

Affirmative

1 I go to school by bus. (we) ....So do we,...
2 He plays the guitar. (I)
3 They live near Verona. (he)
4 I'm watching a football match on TV. (we)
5 We're going to Spain for our holidays. (my parents)

Negative

6 Eddie isn't playing very well.
   (Adam) .Neither/Nor is Adam...
7 I don't want any coffee, thank you. (I)
8 I'm not going out this evening. (she)
9 She doesn't go to our school. (he)
10 I'm not going to stay up late tonight. (I)

Grammar focus

Agreeing with affirmative statements

I'm playing in the match.
So am I. (= I'm playing in the match too.)

Adam's playing in the match.
So is Eddie. (= Eddie's playing in the match too.)

I like Tommaso.
So do I. (= I like him too.)

Rachel likes going to the cinema.
So does Becky. (= Becky likes going to the cinema too.)

Agreeing with negative statements

I'm not hungry.	He isn't tired.
Neither/Nor am I.	**Nor is she.**
I don't like getting up early.	She doesn't speak French.
Neither/Nor do I.	**Nor does he.**

Speak

15a Work with a partner. Use the phrases in the box to ask and answer questions.

> ~~go to dance classes~~   do gymnastics
> collect stamps   like chocolate
> speak German   like getting up early
> play football   read in bed
> play the piano

> A Do you go to dance classes?

> B Yes, I do./No, I don't. Do you?

15b Talk about three things you have in common.

> A I go to dance classes.

> B So do I.

> A I don't collect stamps.

> B Neither do I.

Listen

16 Listen to the conversation three times.
1 Write the letter of the correct picture.
2 Write the location.
3 Write the kit or equipment mentioned.

There are eight conversations.

Picture	Location	Kit/Equipment
1 d	golf course	golf clubs

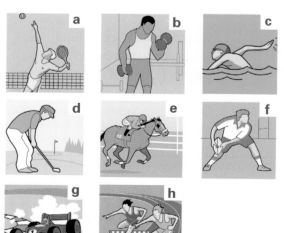

Talk time

17 Complete the sentences with the correct phrase. Then listen and check.

> Well played!   Good luck!   ~~Shut up!~~
> Well done!   See you there.

1 **A** Where's my baseball cap? You've got it!
   B No, I haven't.
   C ..Shut up!.............. I'm trying to work.
2 You've got 10 out of 10 in the Maths test.
   ....
3 **A** We're meeting at Nathan's house at 8.
   B OK. ....
4 **A** I'm swimming in a competition on Saturday.
   B ....
5 Congratulations! You're the winner.
   ....

Remember you can use the Present continuous to talk about future plans:
We're playing in the match this afternoon.
You can use *going to* + verb to talk about firm intentions:
We're going to watch your match.

 Extra!

18 Write three things you're going to do to improve your life. Then write three things you're doing this week.

> I'm going to eat more fruit.................
> I'm not going to stay up late...............
> I'm playing volleyball tomorrow.............

At the disco

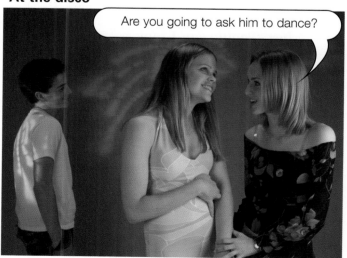

Are you going to ask him to dance?

Skills development

A star at 15

Lorna Want is from Coventry, in the Midlands*. She goes to the Heart of England School. She's a typical girl of 15. She likes the TV programme *Friends*, she loves spending money and she adores shopping. In her bedroom, there are posters of Jennifer Aniston. Lorna admires her. 'People say I look a bit like her.'

But Lorna's real passion is for performing on stage. At the moment, she's living in London and she isn't at school. Why? Because she's playing Juliet in a rock opera version of *Romeo and Juliet* at the Piccadilly Theatre.

Romeo and Juliet is set in Verona, like the original Shakespeare play. It's the hottest ticket in town, so the theatre is full every night. The reason is very simple: people come out of the theatre and say, 'You must see it.'

Lorna isn't alone in London. 'My mum, Christine, is here,' she says. 'So is my brother, James. Unfortunately, my dad, Tony, isn't here. He's at home, but we see him at weekends. He's so proud of me. This is my first big part. Every young girl wants to play Juliet. It's very romantic.'

Unlike Juliet, Lorna hasn't got a boyfriend. 'But when I'm on stage, I look at Romeo and I love him. I am the part.'

What about her school work while she's in London? She has a private tutor and she has lessons in the mornings. She's taking her GCSE* exams next year, so she can't miss lessons!

---

* the Midlands – a region in the middle of England   * GCSE – General Certificate of Secondary Education

Read

1 Read the article about Lorna Want.

2 Complete the chart.

Name .Lorna Want..

School ....

Age ....

Home (usually) ....

Where is she at the moment? ....

Why? ....

Family ..Mum (Christine)..............................

Part in *Romeo and Juliet* ....

Vocabulary

3 Choose the correct meaning for each phrase.

1 She's a fairly typical girl of 15.
  a) She's like a lot of other 15-year-old girls. ✓
  b) She isn't like other 15-year-old girls. ☐

2 Lorna admires her.
  a) She likes her a lot. ☐
  b) She doesn't like her at all. ☐

3 her real passion
  a) something she hates doing ☐
  b) something she really enjoys doing ☐

4 the hottest ticket in town
  a) the most expensive show in town ☐
  b) the most popular show in town ☐

5 He's so proud of me.
  a) He's very pleased about what I'm doing. ☐
  b) He's nervous about what I'm doing. ☐

6 a private tutor
  a) someone who teaches students outside school ☐
  b) a computer which can teach ☐

Listen

4 Listen to a newspaper reporter phoning with information about Lorna Want. She makes five mistakes. What are they? Make notes as you listen. Then write complete sentences. Listen two or three times if necessary.

1 London ✗   Coventry ✓

Lorna isn't from London. She's from Coventry.

2 ....

3 ....

4 ....

5 ....

Speak

5 Work with a partner. Ask and answer about Lorna.

Partner A   **Partner B**
1 Where is Lorna from?

She's from Coventry, in the Midlands.

2 How old is she?
3 What's her favourite TV programme?
4 What does she like doing in her free time?
5 What has she got in her bedroom?

Partner B   **Partner A**
6 Where is Lorna living at the moment?

She's living in London.

7 What is she doing there?
8 Are all her family with her?
9 Why is Lorna different from Juliet?
10 Why is next year important?

Write

6 Rewrite the first paragraph of the article as if it's about you or someone you know.

Adam/Agata is from Gdansk in the north of Poland.

1 Let's check

Vocabulary check

1 **Match the words to make sports equipment.**

	football	[b]	**a**	bat
1	baseball	[ ]	**b**	boots
2	golf	[ ]	**c**	goggles
3	swimming	[ ]	**d**	club
4	swimming	[ ]	**e**	racket
5	tennis	[ ]	**f**	costume

Write your score: …/5

2 **Match the words to make sports locations.**

	golf	[f]	**a**	track
1	baseball	[ ]	**b**	pool
2	football	[ ]	**c**	court
3	athletics	[ ]	**d**	pitch
4	swimming	[ ]	**e**	field
5	tennis	[ ]	**f**	course

Write your score: …/5

Grammar check

3 **Correct the mistake in each sentence.**
/\ = there's a word missing; X = change one word; ⤶ = change the order of two words; * = you must delete one word.

She play the guitar in her free time. **X**
She plays the guitar in her free time.
....

1 Are you going watch the match this afternoon? **/**
....
....

2 My brother doesn't like golf and neither I do. **⤶**
....
....

3 She lives in California and so do I also. *****
....
....

4 Are you playing in the match in this afternoon? *****
....
....

5 They lives near a golf course. **X**
....
....

Write your score: …/5

4 **Circle the correct words for each sentence.**

"I don't like packing." "Neither ..do I..... "
  A I do   **B** am I   **C** do I

1 "We're going to buy some presents." "So …"
  A are we   **B** we do   **C** do we

2 They … meeting her at the café at four.
  A do   **B** going   **C** are

3 "My mum doesn't eat chocolate." " … mine."
  A So does   **B** Neither does **C** Neither is

4 I … the piano every day next week.
  A practising   **B** practise   **C** am going to practise

5 "Alice is very sporty." "… Sue."
  A So does   **B** Neither is   **C** So is

6 They … get home until seven o'clock.
  A doesn't   **B** aren't   **C** don't

7 "My parents hate motorbikes." "… mine."
  A So are   **B** Neither do   **C** So do

8 She … come from Colombia. She's Spanish.
  A doesn't   **B** isn't   **C** not

9 "Their goggles aren't here." " … ours."
  A Neither are   **B** So are   **C** Neither is

10 Why … holding your leg like that?
  A do you   **B** you're   **C** are you

Write your score: …/

5 **Make sentences by putting the words in order.**

at / do / Dean / doesn't / gymnastics / school
Dean doesn't do gymnastics at school.
....

1 always / breakfast / chocolate / Do / eat / for / you / ?
....
....

2 and / is / going / I / Lucy / now / out / so am
....
....

3 are / at / looking / my / skirt / tennis / Why / you / ?
....
....

4 a / Are / buy / car / going / new / parents / to / your / ?
....
....

5 coming / isn't / match / My / sister / the / to / today
....
....

Write your score: …/5
Write your total score: …/30

2

Transport

1a Listen and follow. 🎧

1 bus

2 coach

3 train

4 plane

5 lorry

6 van

7 car

8 taxi/cab

9 motorbike

10 scooter

11 bike

12 ship

13 boat

14 ferry

1b Which of these do you use
- every day?
- at weekends?
- to go on holiday?

2 Listen and point to the signs. 🎧

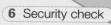

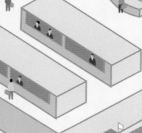

12 Passport control

11 Baggage reclaim

9 Information point

4 ARRIVALS

10 Passengers with hand luggage only

8 Gates

3 DEPARTURES

7 Airlines

2 TERMINAL 1

15 Exit

6 Security check

5 Check-in desk

14 Entrance

❶ Welcome to Stansted Airport

13 Bus stop

2

We have to check in at 2.15

🎧 Listen and read

1 Listen and read.

- *must*, revision
- *have to*
- Past simple of *be*, revision
- Past simple of regular and irregula verbs, revision
- Past continuous, revision
- Talking about jobs around the hou

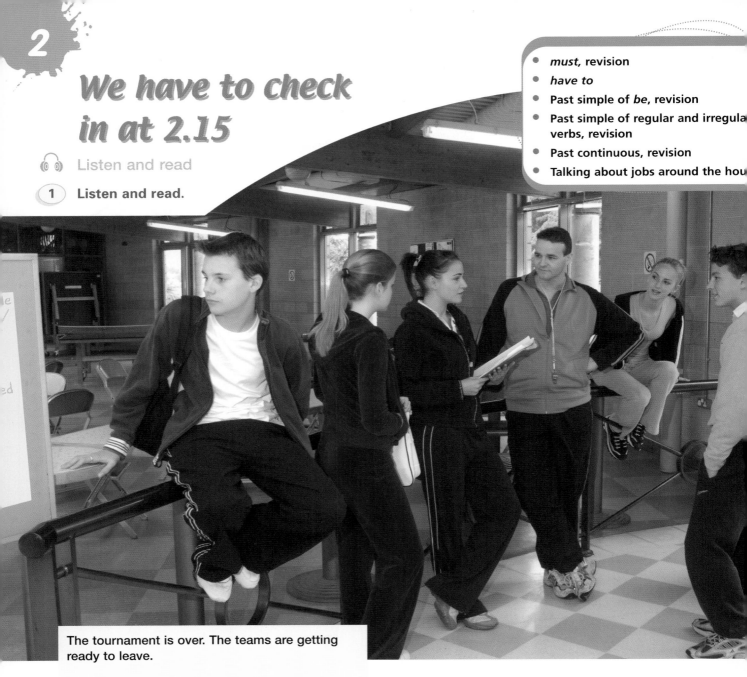

The tournament is over. The teams are getting ready to leave.

Becky	Will there be time to buy presents?
Sally	Yes, but you must do your packing straight after breakfast.
Mike	We have to be at the airport at 2 o'clock. We mustn't be late. We have to check in at 2.15.
Eddie	I hope we're going to have time for lunch.
Adam	Don't panic, Eddie. Look, it says lunch is at 12.30.
Becky	Come on, let's go and pack. Then we can go shopping. I must buy something for my mum.
Eddie	I don't want to go shopping.
Becky	Well, you don't have to come with us.
Rachel	Eddie, you must buy some presents to take home.
Eddie	All right, then. Anyway, it won't take me long to pack. See you here in five minutes.

Comprehension

2 Complete the notice with the words below.

Packing	Check in	Arrive at the airport
~~Breakfast~~	Lunch	

7.30	Breakfast ....
8.30	....
9.30–11.30	Free time (shopping etc.)
12.30	....
1.30	Coach to the airport
2.00	....
2.15	....
4.00	Flight leaves for London

Grammar focus

have to

Affirmative

I/You/We/They have to (leave).

He/She/It has to (leave).

Negative

I/You/We/They don't have to (leave).

He/She/It doesn't have to (leave).

Questions

Do I/you/we/they have to (leave)?

Does he/she/it have to (leave)?

Use *have to* to talk about obligations.

Use *don't have to* to say that something is not necessary.

® *must/mustn't*

I/You/He/She/It/We/You/They must (buy some presents).

Use *must* to talk about your own feelings and wishes.

I/You/He/She/It/We/You/They mustn't (be late).

Use *mustn't* to tell somebody not to do something.

Find examples of each structure in the dialogue.

You can say *I have to* or *I've got to*:
I have to go now.
I've got to go now.

Grammar practice

3 **Complete the sentences.**

have to/has to

don't have to/doesn't have to

1 There's no school today so you ..don't.have.to... get up early.

2 The journey to school takes an hour. She .... leave home at 6.45 a.m.

3 I'm taking a piano exam next month so I .... practise every evening.

4 We're going shopping but you .... come if you don't want to.

5 You can't buy tickets on the train. You .... buy them at the station.

Speak

4 **Work with a partner. Ask and answer about what you have to do at home. Use the prompts below.**

A What sort of things do you have to do at home?

B I have to tidy my room and I have to take the dog for a walk.

A Do you have to help with the shopping?

- clean the car
- take the dog for a walk
- cook the supper
- do the washing up
- clear the table
- help with the shopping
- tidy my room
- make my bed
- take the rubbish out
- hang out the washing

Write

5 **Write two sentences about**
- **what you have to do at home**
- **what your brother/sister/best friend has to do at home.**

Talk time

6a **Complete the sentences with the correct phrases.**

I hope	Don't panic	See you
straight after	~~It says~~	

1 Oh, no. Look at the Departures board. ....It says....... the plane's two hours late.

2 .... at the cinema at 7.30.

3 .... it's going to be sunny tomorrow.

4 ...., everything's OK.

5 Let's go to the pool .... school.

6b **Work with a partner. Write new sentences using the phrases in the box.**

Look at that notice. It says there's a free concert in the park next Saturday.

2

🎧 Listen and read

7 **Listen and read.**

Sally	Hi, everybody! So what did you do this morning?
Rachel	We took the bus into town. We went straight to the shops. They were brilliant.
Becky	I bought some perfume for my mum.
Rachel	I found a lovely poster of Verona for my mum and dad.
Becky	Eddie got some chocolates and Adam bought some biscuits.
Rachel	We saw the famous balcony.
Becky	But we didn't see Romeo.
Eddie	Or Juliet.
Adam	We had cakes and hot chocolate in a café.
Sally	Did you ask for them in English?
Eddie	No, we didn't, actually.
Rachel	We asked Tommaso and he told us what to say.

Comprehension

8a **Match the person to the present.**

Becky ......c........................ Eddie ....

Rachel .... Adam ....

8b **Answer the questions.**

1 Where did Rachel, Becky, Adam and Eddie go?

They went into town.......
2 How did they get there?
3 Did Sally go with them?
4 What did they do first?
5 What did they see?
6 What did they have in the café?
7 Who was with them?

22

Grammar focus

The Past simple of *be*

Affirmative

I was
You/We/They were
He/She/It was
} (in *Verona*).

How do you form the negative of *be* in the Past simple? How do you form Past simple questions with *be*?

The Past simple of regular verbs

Add **ed** or **d** to the infinitive:
ask – ask**ed**, like – like**d**
We asked Tommaso for help.

For the Past simple of irregular verbs, see page 135.

How many verbs in the Past simple can you find in the dialogue?

Grammar practice

9 Use the chart to write six true sentences about what you did last weekend.

I watched a good film. I didn't play football.

Regular verbs	
watch	a good film
listen to	a CD
cycle	an interesting book
play	a nice meal
help	basketball
phone	football
	in the house
	to the park
Irregular verbs	into town
go	music
see	my/your friends
have	my homework
do	to the cinema
buy	TV
read	volleyball

Speak

10a Work with a partner. Ask and answer about the weekend.

A What did you do at the weekend?

B I played basketball on Saturday morning.

10b Tell someone else in the class what your partner did at the weekend.

Extra!

11 Write an account of the week in Italy. Use Rachel's diary to help you.

On Sunday, they left Stansted at 2.30. It was cold! They arrived in Verona ....

Sunday
Leave Stansted at 2.30 p.m. – cold. Arrive in Verona at 4.30 p.m. – hot.

Monday
Go to the Welcome Party. Meet players from other teams.

Tuesday
a.m.: play our first match. The score: England 1 Germany 0. p.m.: the boys play their first match.

Wednesday
Play our second match. Score: England 1 Argentina 3.

Thursday
Have a rest day. Go swimming.

Friday
Play our last match. Go to disco!

Saturday
Buy some presents. Take some photos.

Sally — Eddie, where were you?

Rachel — We nearly missed the plane.

Eddie — Sorry! I was in the shop.

Module 1
23
Unit 2

2

Listen and read.

12 **Listen and read.**

At the airport

Mum	Did you have a good time?
Eddie	Yes, we had a great time. It was brilliant!
Becky	But we nearly missed the plane. We were all waiting at the gate in departures but Eddie wasn't there.
Rachel	We were really worried.
Eddie	I was buying presents in the shop. They called me over the tannoy but I wasn't listening.
Mum	Well, never mind. You're here now. Anyway, while you were playing in the tournament, the sports reporter from the *Evening News* phoned.
Adam	Really?
Mum	His name's Steve Turner. That's him over there. He was waiting here when I arrived.
Eddie	Yeah! We're famous!

Grammar focus

R **Past continuous**

Affirmative

I was waiting
He/She/It was waiting   } (at the gate).
We/You/They were waiting

Do you remember the negative and question forms?

Complete the sentences.

I was laughing. (I/cry/✗) I wasn't crying.

You were riding your bike. (You/walk/✗) ....

(He/sing/✗) .... He was shouting.

(you/talk/?) Were you talking. to Becky when I phoned?

(they/win/?) .... at half-time?

(she/go/?) .... to the swimming pool when you saw her?

How many examples of the Past continuous can you find in the dialogue?

Comprehension

13 **Answer the questions.**

1 How did the team travel from Verona to London?
  By plane.....

2 Who was late?

3 Where was he?

4 What did he buy?

5 Who phoned Eddie's mum?

While

While you were playing in the tournament, a reporter phoned.

A reporter phoned while you were playing in the tournament.

When

When I arrived, he was waiting here.

He was waiting here when I arrived.

Grammar practice

14 **Complete the sentences with the verb in the Past continuous.**

Affirmative

1 I (have) ...*was having*... a shower when you phoned.
2 They (watch) .... TV when I arrived.
3 While he (read) .... the newspaper, the dog ate his dinner.
4 While you (do) .... your homework, I made you a cake.

Negative

5 You (not listen) *weren't listening*.. when the teacher told us what to do.
6 My dad (not watch) .... when I scored a goal.
7 They (not wait) .... at the airport when I arrived.
8 I (not be horrible) .... when I left the party early.

Questions

9 Where (they/go) ..*were they going*.... when you saw them?
10 (you/watch) .... *Friends* when I phoned?
11 What (you/think about) .... when you started to laugh?
12 (he/wear) .... that silly hat when you saw him?

 Listen

15 **Listen and write the letters of the activities each person was doing.**

1 Jessica ...*c*.............   2 Nicole ....

3 Katie ....   4 Luke ....

5 William ....   6 Ryan ....

 Pronunciation

Same letters, different sounds

16a **Listen to the differences between the vowel sounds in these words.**

1	b<u>i</u>ke	b<u>i</u>scuit
2	f<u>a</u>mily	f<u>a</u>mous
3	h<u>ea</u>r	<u>ea</u>rly
4	t<u>ow</u>n	kn<u>ow</u>
5	g<u>oe</u>s	d<u>oe</u>s
6	y<u>our</u>	j<u>our</u>ney

16b **Find a word in the chart with the same vowel sound as:**

1 <u>o</u>nly ....*know*..........   2 l<u>a</u>te ....
3 t<u>ou</u>rnament ....   4 n<u>ea</u>rly....................
5 n<u>ow</u> ....   6 t<u>i</u>me ....

 Extra!

17 **Ask and answer with a partner.**

What were you doing:
yesterday morning at 7.30?

> I was having breakfast/a shower.

yesterday afternoon at 4.30?
yesterday evening at 8 o'clock?

on (Saturday) morning at 10.00?
on (Saturday) afternoon at 2.30?
on (Saturday) evening at 9.30?

Write

18 **Write what your partner was doing yesterday and on the other day you chose.**

Yesterday morning at 7.30 Daniela was listening to the radio. ....

Portfolio

19 **Write an e-mail to a friend describing a recent trip. Go to page 128.**

Skills development

A Junior World Cup

Read

1 **Read the text about a football tournament.**

The opening ceremony for the International Junior Football Tournament took place in the centre of Barcelona. Teams from twenty different countries took part.

'We walked with our flags through the streets and sang songs in many different languages,' said Emily Hanson, from the British team. 'It was really exciting.'

'We played on pitches next to Barcelona's Olympic Stadium,' said Hannah Forster, another member of the British team. 'It was like the Olympics. It was a real international event.'

The players didn't find the mixture of languages a problem. 'We just used a sort of sign language,' explained Hannah.

'We played Brazil first and they were really good. They won 4-1. But then we played Mexico and we won 4-1,' said Jordan Bowes, from the UK boys' team. The boys played Denmark next and won 11-2. 'So we were getting better!' laughed Jordan. Their next game was against Argentina. They had to win to get to the quarter finals. 'We were playing really well, but when the final whistle blew, the score was Argentina 4, UK 1.'

2 **Complete the match results.**

Boys' team	Team 1		Team 2	
Match 1	UK	1	Brazil	4
Match 2	UK			
Match 3	UK			
Match 4	UK			

Girls' team	Team 1		Team 2	
Semi-final	UK			

Tournament winners

Boys:

Girls:

Vocabulary

3 **Look at the context for each of these words or phrases. Can you work out what they mean?**

1 the opening ceremony
2 (it) took place in (the centre of Barcelona)
3 (they) took part in (a tournament)
4 a real international event
5 the mixture of languages
6 sign language
7 when the final whistle blew
8 a tough match
9 (they) were disappointed
10 the lads

The British girls got to the semi–finals and played the USA. It was a tough match. They lost 7-1.

The two British teams were disappointed not to get to the finals but they enjoyed their stay in Spain. 'The whole trip was fantastic,' said Rikardo Reid, 12, from Birmingham. 'The lads out there were good, really friendly.'

The winners of the tournament were the boys' team from Israel and the girls' team from America.

Speak

5 Imagine you are at the tournament in Barcelona. Ask the questions in Exercise 4. Choose your answers from the pictures.

A When did you leave (Lisbon)?

B We left .... days ago.

Write

6 Write a report of a match you played in or a match you've seen. It can be any sport. Answer these questions first:

Where did the match take place?
Who was playing?
What was the match like?
Who was winning at half-time?
Who won the match?

The match between ... and .... took place in ....

 Listen

4 Listen and tick (✓) the correct answers.

1 When did you leave London?

   a 3 days ago ☐

   b 7 days ago ☐

   c 10 days ago ✓

2 How did you travel to Barcelona?

   a ☐

   b ☐

   c ☐

   d ☐

3 What did you bring with you?

   a ☐    **d** ☐

   b ☐    **e** ☐

   c ☐    **f** ☐

4 What did you enjoy most about the tournament?

   a eating Spanish paella ☐

   b making lots of new friends from different countries ☐

   c going to the beach ☐

Culture spot

William Shakespeare (1564-1616)

🎧 Listen and read

1 Listen to and read the text about William Shakespeare. Then complete the picture captions.

The most famous English writer is William Shakespeare and *Romeo and Juliet* is his most famous play. It's set in Italy, but Shakespeare never went there. In fact, he probably never left England.

Shakespeare came from Stratford-on-Avon, in the Midlands. You can still visit the house where Shakespeare was born. He lived in Stratford-on-Avon with his wife, Anne Hathaway, and his children, Susanna, Judith and Hamnet.

Shakespeare was an actor as well as a writer. He appeared in his own plays at The Globe and other London theatres. He also performed at the Royal Palaces, in front of Queen Elizabeth I. He wrote nearly forty plays as well as sonnets and other poems.

Going to the theatre was very popular in Shakespeare's time. It wasn't just for the rich. You could go to a play at The Globe for just one penny. You didn't have a seat but you stood very close to the stage so you had a very good view of the action.

1 The ....**musicians**.... played in the gallery above the ....

2 Shakespeare was born in this ....

3 A scene from the film *Shakespeare in Love*: This is Queen .... I.

4 The .... Theatre is on the south bank of the River ....

The audience expected to hear music, too, as part of the play. At The Globe the musicians played in a gallery above the stage.

Women didn't appear on stage in Shakespeare's time. So boys played the women's parts. Theatres were lively places. The audience didn't keep quiet during the performance.

Unfortunately the old Globe Theatre burnt down a long time ago. But there is a new Globe Theatre on the south bank of the River Thames. It looks exactly like the old one. You can go and see Shakespeare's plays there now.

5 .... is Shakespeare's most famous play.

Vocabulary

2a **Find the words for:**

1 a type of poem
2 a small amount of money in Shakespeare's time
3 people who watch a play
4 a person who performs in a play
5 people who have a lot of money

2b **Can you guess what the underlined words mean?**

1 It's <u>set</u> in Verona.
2 He probably never <u>left</u> England.
3 You didn't have a <u>seat</u>.
4 You <u>stood</u> very close to the stage.
5 Theatres were <u>lively</u> places.
6 The audience didn't <u>keep quiet</u> during the performance.
7 The old Globe Theatre <u>burnt down</u> a long time ago.

Comprehension

3 **Answer the questions.**

1 Who is William Shakespeare?
   He's the most famous English writer.
2 When did he live?
3 Where did he come from?
4 What was his wife's name?
5 How many children did he have?
6 Who was Queen during Shakespeare's time?
7 Who played the women's parts in Shakespeare's plays?
8 Where is the new Globe Theatre?

Write

4 **Write four questions about a famous writer. Then write the answers.**

Where did ... come from?
He/She came from ...

Let's check

Vocabulary check

1 **Match the transport words to the sentences.**

bus	motorbike	taxi
ferry	~~plane~~	van

It flies. ...plane....

1 It takes people and cars across the sea. ....
2 It's like a scooter but it's bigger usually. ....
3 It's like a small lorry and carries things. ....
4 You get on and off it at stops. ....
5 You pay the driver of this car. ....

Write your score: .../5

Grammar check

2 **Correct the mistake in each sentence.**

/\ = there's a word missing; X = change one word; ↪ = change the order of two words; * = you must delete one word.

You wasn't listening to my story. X
You weren't listening to my story. ....

1 You didn't made your bed this morning. X

....

2 Why you did take my tennis racket? ↪

....

3 We don't have got to get up early tomorrow. *

....

4 What you doing at seven o'clock yesterday evening? /\

....

5 We must to go to the check-in desk now. *

....

6 Where was you last night? X

....

7 What were you doing when I phoned? ↪

....

8 What we have to do? /\

....

9 They didn't saw their friend last weekend. X

....

10 We mustn't to be late. *

....

Write your score: ..../10

3 **Choose the correct words for each sentence.**

I .found. my glasses under my bed yesterday.
A find B finding C found

1 You don't ... wear white for tennis.
A must B need C have to

2 You must ... park here.
A not B to C have

3 We ... win the match.
A didn't B weren't C aren't

4 She ... a poster for me in France last summer.
A buys B bought C was buying

5 What ... you about the tournament?
A she did tell B she told C did she tell

6 We ... worried about the test.
A was B were C did

7 Why were you ... yesterday?
A cry B crying C cried

8 "I bought a CD today." "So ... I."
A was B do C did

9 I have ... my room this afternoon.
A to tidy B tidying C tidy

10 My mum ... me some perfume.
A buy B bought C buying

Write your score: ..../10

4 **Make sentences by putting the words in order.**

didn't / morning / hang / out / the / this / washing / You
You didn't hang out the washing this morning. ......

1 boots / Why / wearing / were / yesterday / you ?

....

2 dog / for / got / She's / take / the / to / a walk

....

3 have / help / me / shopping / the / to / today / with / You

....

4 and / I / Anna / after / any / chocolates / didn't / dinner / eat

....

5 a drink / and / bought / the café / Ella / in / a / me / cake

....

Write your score: ..../5
Write your total score: ..../30

How good are you?

★ I'm not very good at this. ★/★ I'm OK at this. ★★★ I'm good at this.

Tick (✓) the correct boxes.

		★	★/★	★★★
READING I can understand:				
a dialogue about a match	*He's playing really well. Come on, Eddie, you aren't running!*			
a dialogue about plans for later	*Are you going to the disco this evening? Yes, see you there.*			
an article about a young actor	*She's playing Juliet in a rock opera version of Romeo and Juliet.*			
an article about the Junior World Cup	*We walked with our flags through the streets.*			
an article about Shakespeare	*Going to the theatre was very popular in Shakespeare's time.*			
LISTENING I can understand:				
people giving information about themselves	*Where do you live? I live in Cambridge. What are your favourite subjects? I like Music.*			
people planning sports activities	*We're going to stay at a hotel with six tennis courts.*			
a phone report about a young actor	*The star of the rock opera Romeo and Juliet is Lorna Want.*			
an interview with a young team member	*How did you travel to Barcelona? Did you come all the way by coach?*			
WRITING I can write:				
a list of resolutions	*I'm going to eat more fruit.*			
a list of future plans	*I'm playing volleyball tomorrow.*			
a report about a match	*At half-time we were winning. Then the Dolphins scored a goal.*			
questions and answers about a famous writer	*Where did Pushkin come from? Pushkin came from Moscow.*			
SPEAKING I can:				
give people's personal details	*Matthew is 13. He lives in Cambridge.*			
talk about what's happening in a match	*He's running towards the goal.*			
talk about things I have in common with someone	*I like chocolate. So do I. I'm not very good at skiing. Nor am I.*			
role-play a reporter and a team member	*When did you leave Lisbon? We left … days ago.*			

Vocabulary groups

Write three more words in each vocabulary group.

Sports kit	trainers	shorts	T-shirt	....	....	....
Sports equipment	ball	....	....	....		
Sports locations	gym	tennis court	....	....	....	
Transport	car	bus	bike	....	....	....

Grammar

Present perfect simple

Present perfect simple with *ever* and *never*

been and *gone*

Present perfect with *just, already* and *yet*

Present perfect with *for* and *since*

Present perfect and Past simple contrasted

Vocabulary

Communications

Films and plays

Communication

Talk about experiences

Relating past experiences to periods of time

Pronunciation

The letter *r* at the beginning and end of words

Stressed syllables

Culture spot

School swap

3

Communications

3   envelope

1 Listen and say what the words are in your language. 🎧

1   post office

2   letter

4   postcard

6   address

5   stamp

7   postcode

8   post box

2a Listen and follow. 🎧

Emergency services:

1   mobile phone ✓

2   directory enquiries ☐

3   international code ☐

4   fire ☐

5   police ☐

6   ambulance ☐

2b Listen to the conversations and tick (✓) the words and phrases you hear. 🎧

3a Are any of the following words the same or similar in your language?

1   e-mail
2   message
3   e-mail address
4   the internet/the net
5   website

3b Now listen to them. 🎧

4 Translate these phrases.

1   to post a letter
2   to send a letter/an e-mail/a text message
3   to get a letter/an e-mail/a phone call from someone
4   to ring/phone/call someone
5   to check your messages
6   to leave a message
7   to check your e-mails
8   to surf the net

We've had an e-mail from Tommaso

Listen and read

1 **Listen and read.**

It's October 31st. Becky is having a Hallowe'en party at her house. She's invited some friends from school and from Cambridge Juniors Football Club.

8 p.m.

Becky	Where are Adam and Eddie?
Rachel	They've gone to Eddie's house to get ready.

An hour later

Becky	Oh, you're here at last!
Adam	We've walked all the way from Eddie's house.
Eddie	And we've frightened lots of people on the way! Ha, ha!
Rachel	Guess what? I've had an e-mail from Tommaso. He's started at a new school.
Eddie	Oh, why? What's he done wrong?
Becky	He hasn't done anything wrong! His father's changed jobs and they've moved to Milan.
Adam	Does he like it there?
Rachel	Yes, I think so. He's made some new friends and he's joined a football team.
Adam	I've had a postcard from Eloisa – you know, from the Mexican team.
Becky	Ooh!
Adam	She's been to Acapulco on holiday.
Eddie	I haven't heard from anybody!
Becky	Well, I bet you haven't written to anybody.
Eddie	That's true.

Comprehension

2 **Answer the questions.**

1 What's happening at Becky's house?
   She's having a Hallowe'en party.
2 Who arrive late?
3 Who is the e-mail from, and who is it to?
4 Where is Tommaso now?
5 Who is Adam's postcard from?

Grammar focus

To make the Present perfect simple, use the present tense of **have** + the **past participle** of the verb.

I've   walked

Past participles are either regular or irregular.
Regular past participles end in **ed** or **d**:

   walk**ed**
   mov**ed**

Irregular past participles ... you just have to learn them!

make → made   have → had

Find more examples of regular and irregular past participles in the dialogue.

Present perfect simple

Affirmative		Negative	
I've	(walked).	I haven't	(walked).
You've		You haven't	
He's/She's/It's		He/She/It hasn't	
We've		We haven't	
You've		You haven't	
They've		They haven't	

Grammar practice

3 Complete the sentences with the Present perfect of the verbs in brackets.

Affirmative

1 (invite) I 've invited....... Chiara and Ilaria to my party. I hope they can come.

2 (start) The film .... Be quiet!

3 (do) I .... my homework. Can I go out now?

4 (write) Joe .... to Sarah three times this week. He really likes her.

5 (have) We .... four tests this week. It's not fair!

Negative

1 (change) I can't go out now. I haven't changed........ my clothes.

2 (invite) You .... Briony to your party. Why not?

3 (have) Sorry, I .... time to tidy my room.

4 (hear) Eddie .... from anybody.

5 (write) He .... to anybody.

Be careful! The verb **go** has two past participles.

*They've **gone** to Eddie's house.*
(= They went to Eddie's house and they're still there.)

*She's **been** to Acapulco.*
(= She went to Acapulco and she's now back home.)

4 Complete the sentences with **been** or **gone**.

1 'Why don't you want to come to the cinema?'
'Because we've .been.... to the cinema three times this week.'

2 'Where's Ella?'
'She's .... to the swimming pool.'

3 'You're very brown.'
'I've .... to Tenerife on holiday.'

4 'Are George and Patrick coming to the park?'
'No, they've .... to the shops'.

5 'Let's go to York for the day.'
'Good idea. We haven't .... there.'

Speak

5 Tell your partner three things you've done this week. One of the things is not true. Your partner has to guess which one.

Write your sentences first. Use these verbs:

Regular	Irregular
play	go
watch	do
walk	make

A I've played basketball. I've been to the beach. I've walked to school every day.

B You haven't been to the beach.

A Correct./No, I haven't walked to school every day.

6 Play the game again, using other verbs. You'll find a list of irregular verbs on page 135.

Listen and read

7 **Listen and read.**

Eddie   Have you had another e-mail from Tommaso?
Rachel Yes, we have. Do you want to read it?

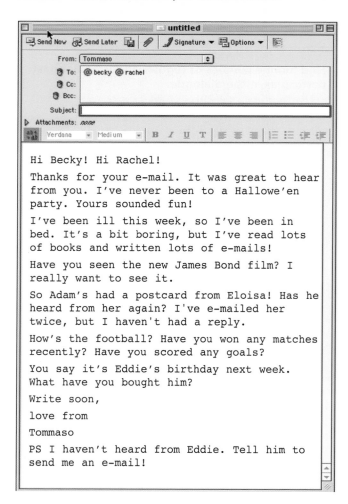

Hi Becky! Hi Rachel!

Thanks for your e-mail. It was great to hear from you. I've never been to a Hallowe'en party. Yours sounded fun!

I've been ill this week, so I've been in bed. It's a bit boring, but I've read lots of books and written lots of e-mails!

Have you seen the new James Bond film? I really want to see it.

So Adam's had a postcard from Eloisa! Has he heard from her again? I've e-mailed her twice, but I haven't had a reply.

How's the football? Have you won any matches recently? Have you scored any goals?

You say it's Eddie's birthday next week. What have you bought him?

Write soon,

love from

Tommaso

PS I haven't heard from Eddie. Tell him to send me an e-mail!

How many times?
1 = once
2 = twice
3 = three times

Comprehension

8 **Look at the pictures. Tick (✓) the things Tommaso has done this week.**

a ☐   b ☐   c ☐

d ✔   e ☐   f ☐

Grammar focus

Present perfect simple
Questions

Have I	(played)?
Have you/we/they	
Has he/she/it	

Short answers

Affirmative	**Negative**
Yes, I/you/we/they have.	No, I/you/we/they haven't.
Yes, he/she/it has.	No, he/she/it hasn't.

9a Complete the questions with the correct question word and *have/has*.

what	which	where
why	~~who~~	how

1 ....Who has....... sent a postcard to Adam?
2 .... you been?
3 .... he done?
4 .... she been late every day this week?
5 .... *Harry Potter* books .... you read?
6 .... many books .... you read more than once?

Grammar practice

9b Complete the questions and short answers.

1
(you)
..Have you had.. a postcard from Eloisa?
Yes, I have.............

2
(they)
....
football this week?
Yes, they ....

3
(you)
.... the new James Bond film?
No, I ....

4
(he)
....
any e-mails today?
Yes, he ....

5
(she)
.... any good books recently?
Yes, she ....

6
(you)
.... to any parties recently?
No, we ....

Do you remember?
The verb *go* has two past participles: *gone* and ....
Been is also the past participle of the verb *be*: *I've been ill*.

10a Are you a good communicator? Work with a partner. Ask and answer about last week. Record your partner's answers.

In the last three days ...

Have you
1 sent any postcards?
2 written any letters?
3 sent any text messages?
4 had any faxes?
5 found any good websites?
6 been to the post office?

How many times have you
7 used a mobile phone?
8 surfed the net?
9 phoned your best friend?
10 checked your e-mail?

10b Write sentences about you and your partner.

In the last three days I haven't sent any postcards but I've sent lots of text messages. My partner has written a letter to her pen-friend.

Talk time

11a Match the questions and answers. Then listen and check.

1 Guess what? ....b......
2 What's he done wrong?
3 Where did you see Miranda?
4 Why is she tired?
5 Regina? Who is Regina?
6 At last! Where have you been?

a He's been late for school every day this week.
b I don't know. Tell me!
c She's cycled all the way from town.
d She was on her way to the swimming pool.
e Sorry, we got lost.
f You know, she's the girl from Brazil.

11b Work with a partner. Think of new answers to the questions in 11a.

1 Guess what?

You've passed your exam.

Read and listen

12a **Match the pictures to the questions.**

a

b

c

d

e

TWENTY QUESTIONS

1 Have you ever climbed a mountain? ......s....
2 Have you ever cooked dinner for your family?
3 Have you ever danced in the street?
4 Have you ever cut your own hair?
5 Have you ever coloured your hair?
6 Have you ever eaten a hot Indian curry?
7 Have you ever been frightened?
8 Have you ever been to another country?
9 Have you ever lived in another country?
10 Have you ever been in a play?
11 Have you ever been on television?
12 Have you ever stayed up all night?
13 Have you ever had chocolate ice cream for breakfast?
14 Have you ever won a competition?
15 Have you ever seen a ghost?
16 Have you ever met anyone famous?
17 Have you ever made a wish that has come true?
18 Have you ever lost your purse or your wallet?
19 Have you ever written a song?
20 Have you ever fallen off a horse?

f

g

h

i

j

k

l

m

n

o

p

q

r

s

t

12b **Now listen to Adam asking Becky the questions. Tick (✓) the things she's done.**

Grammar focus

Present perfect simple with *ever* and *never*

Notice the position of the words *ever* and *never* in these sentences:

Have you **ever** (climbed a mountain)?

I've **never** (climbed a mountain).

How do you say these sentences in your language?

Grammar practice

13a **Write the questions and answers using *ever* and *never*.**

1 you/go/to Britain or the USA?

   <u>Have you ever been to Britain or the USA?</u>

   (✓) Britain   (✗) USA

   <u>I've been to Britain but I've never been to the USA.</u>

2 she/go/skiing or snowboarding?

   ....

   (✓) skiing   (✗) snowboarding

   She ....

3 they/have a cat or a dog?

   ....

   (✗) cat   (✓) dog

   They ....

4 you/write/to a pop singer or a film star?

   ....

   (✓) pop singer   (✗) film star

   I ....

13b **Look at Exercise 12a and complete the chart.**

Base form	Past simple	Past participle
eat	ate	eaten
meet	met	....
make	made	....
fall	fell	....
lose	lost	....
see	saw	....
write	wrote	....
have	had	....

The letter *r* at the beginning and end of words.

14a **Listen and repeat.**

1	Rachel	6	another
2	red	7	ever
3	ready	8	letter
4	ring	9	never
5	rugby	10	singer

14b **In two minutes, how many words can you think of:**

• beginning with r?

• ending in r?

Speak

15a **Work with a partner. Ask and answer the questions in Exercise 12a.**

A Have you ever climbed a mountain?

B Yes, I have.

Record your partner's answers, like this:

1 ✓   2 ✗

15b **Tell the class about your partner.**

A Marek has climbed a mountain. He's never cooked dinner for his family.

Extra!

16 **Write five more questions to ask your partner.**

<u>Have you ever eaten Japanese food?</u>

A lot of English verbs are irregular. The best way to remember them is to learn them by heart, like this:

Base form	Past simple	Past participle
do	did	done
have	had	had
win	won	won

Skills development

Have you ever swum with a crocodile

Read

1 Read the newspaper article about the swimming club.

Comprehension

2 Answer the questions.

1 Where is the Casuarina Crocs Swimming Club?
It's in Darwin, Australia...
2 What's the coach's name?
3 What's different about his training method?
4 Do the swimmers like the new training method? How do you know?
5 How big is the crocodile?
6 How old are the swimmers?
7 Why are some parents unhappy about the method?
8 Why is the crocodile quite friendly?

Vocabulary

3a Can you think of an Italian word which is similar to each of the following?

1 method
2 encourage
3 regularly
4 motivate
5 criticise
6 bizarre

A swimming coach in Darwin, Australia, has found a new training method to encourage his pupils to swim faster. He puts a crocodile in the pool with them.

Mark Davies, from the Casuarina Crocs Swimming Club, has regularly used a crocodile to motivate his senior swimming squad. 'They've become much better swimmers ... and much quicker!'

'Swimming up and down a pool can be quite boring,' says a member of the squad. 'But it's not boring when there's a crocodile in the water!'

'I've noticed a different atmosphere in the club. The children have become a lot closer and they're enjoying life a lot more,' says Mr Davies.

The crocodile is over a metre long. The swimmers, who are between the ages of 13 and 21, can see it under the water. It's free to swim around as it pleases. The swimmers don't race the crocodile. It usually just stays in the shallow water.

Some people don't think it's a good idea. They think it's cruel and they've phoned the pool's manager to complain. The Australian Institute of Sport has criticised Mr Davies. So has the RSPCA*. One of Australia's top swimming coaches, Forbes Carlile, has said, 'It's bizarre, really bizarre. You don't always swim faster when you're frightened.' Parents, too, have been worried. They say it's dangerous.

But Mr Davies is sure that his swimming lessons are safe for both the animal and the swimmers. 'The crocodile has come from the tourist park so it's quite friendly. However, we put tape around the crocodile's mouth and cut its claws, just to be sure. We've never had any problems.'

* Royal Society for the Prevention of Cruelty to Animals

3b **Can you guess the meaning of these words from their context?**

1 training   5 shallow
2 squad   6 complain
3 atmosphere   7 tape
4 race   8 claws

Listen

4 **Listen to the interviews. What do the people think about putting a crocodile in the pool? Tick (✓) the correct boxes.**

	For	Against
1	✓	☐
2	☐	☐
3	☐	☐
4	☐	☐
5	☐	☐

Speak

5 **Read the article and listen to the tape again. What do you think about putting a crocodile in the pool? Prepare your arguments for or against. Then in small groups, say what you think.**

Here are some phrases to help you:

I think it's (dangerous).

I agree./I don't agree.

So do I./Neither do I.

We should .../We shouldn't ...

It should .../It shouldn't ...

Write

6 **Write three or four sentences giving your opinions.**

I think it's cruel to put a crocodile in a swimming pool. It should live in a river. It shouldn't...

3

Let's check

Vocabulary check

1 **Match the words to the sentences.**

ambulance	directory enquiries	e-mails
~~the internet~~	mobile phone	emergency services

You surf it when you are looking for information.
.the. internet..

1 You can put this phone in your pocket or bag.
....

2 They drive people to hospitals in this. ....

3 You phone them when you don't know a telephone number. ....

4 You use the internet to send these letters.
....

5 You call them when you need the police or a doctor, or when there's a fire. ....

Write your score: …/5

2 **Complete the text with the correct words.**

address	~~letter~~	stamp
envelope	post box	postcode

I wrote a .....letter....... to my aunt Louisa in London. I put it in an (1).............. and wrote the (2).............. . The (3).............. was W6 9DY. Then I put a (4)............on it and walked to the (5)............ at the end of my street. I posted my letter to Louisa. She'll probably get it in two days.

Write your score: …/5

Grammar check

3 **Correct the mistake in each sentence. ⋀ = there's a word missing; X = change one word; ↪ = change the order of two words; * = you must delete one word.**

Have ever you written a poem or a song? ↪
Have you ever written a poem or a song?

1 I've been gone to California twice – it's really beautiful. *
....

2 He never been in a school play. ⋀
....

3 What you done with my favourite Shakira CD? ⋀
....

4 Why you have put my shoes in the rubbish? ↪
....

5 Did you ever acted in a school play? X
....

Write your score: …/5

4 **Circle the correct words for each sentence.**

Who has ...eaten.... all the chocolate ice cream?
A ate   **B** eating   **C** eaten ⟵

1 They .... had anything to eat all day.
A have   **B** haven't   **C** didn't

2 We've all .... our names on the list.
A written   **B** wrote   **C** write

3 I can't find my tennis racket. Who .... it?
A did take   **B** has taken   **C** was taking

4 He's .... been on a ship.
A never   **B** ever   **C** will

5 Joey and Beth are out. They've .... to the park.
A been   **B** gone   **C** went

6 .... you heard from Teresa?
A Did   **B** Were   **C** Have

7 Have you ever .... off your motorcycle?
A fallen   **B** fell   **C** fall

8 Why has he .... to bed? It's only seven o'clock.
A been   **B** gone   **C** went

9 My sister has .... all the James Bond movies.
A see   **B** seen   **C** saw

10 Fantastic! We have .... the tournament again.
A win   **B** winning   **C** won

Write your score: …/10

5 **Make sentences by putting the words in ord**

1 a / ever / lost / Has / match / sister / tennis / your / ?
....
....

2 a / lot / letters / of / this / We've / week / written
....
....

3 plane / a / been / has / Maria / never / on
....
....

4 friends / from / Have / Portugal / you heard / in / your / ?
....
....

5 any / hasn't / matches / Our / recently / team / won
....
....

Write your score: …/
Write your total score: …/3

4

Films and plays

1a Listen to these words. Tick (✓) the words that are similar in your language.

1 comedy ✓
2 opera ☐
3 ballet ☐
4 concert ☐
5 musical ☐
6 pantomime ☐
7 play ☐

1b Now check the meaning with your teacher.

1c You're in London for a week. You can go to a play, a film, a concert, a pantomime, an opera, a musical or a ballet. Which are you going to choose? Why?

2a Listen and repeat.

2b Now listen and number the items in the order they're mentioned.

3a Listen and read. What do you think the underlined words mean? Try to guess, then check in your dictionary.

I was in the school play. One of our teachers wrote the script. I played the main character.
I had a lot of lines to learn. We had lots of rehearsals and two dress rehearsals. There were lots of changes of scene. We gave three performances. It was quite a complicated plot but the audience really enjoyed it.

3b Find people in your class who have been in a play. Ask them these questions.

1 Have you ever been in a play? What was it?
2 Which part did you play?
3 Did you wear a costume?
4 Were you one of the main characters?
5 Are you good at learning lines?
6 Are you nervous on stage?
7 Do you know the plot of *Cinderella*? Who are the main characters?
8 Which part would you like to play in *Cinderella*?

a stage ☐
b actor ☐
c actress ☐
d costume ☐
e orchestra ☐
h box office ☐
g audience ☐ 1
j programme ☐
i ticket ☐
f seat ☐

Your wish has just come true!

- Present perfect with *just, already* and *yet*
- Present perfect with *for* and *since*
- Present perfect and Past simple contrasted
- Relating past experiences to periods of time

Listen and read

1 **Listen and read.**

Cambridge Juniors are putting on *Cinderella* for their Christmas pantomime.

At Adam's house

Dad   How are the rehearsals for Cinderella going?

Adam   Quite well.

Dad   Have you learnt your lines yet?

Adam   Yes, Mum helped me with them last weekend.

At Eddie's house

Gran   Eddie, what have you done to your hair?

Eddie   I've sprayed it purple. No, I'm only joking. It's a wig. It's for the pantomime. I'm one of the Ugly Sisters.

Gran   Mmm. What did your dad say?

Eddie   He hasn't seen it yet.

At Rachel's house

Becky   Let's do the poster for the pantomime.

Rachel   I've already done it. I did it this morning. Look!

Becky   Oh, it's lovely!

It's the day of the dress rehearsal.

Becky   I've just seen Eddie. Guess what? He's bought a purple wig!

Rachel   No!

Becky   I can't wait to see him in a dress.

Eddie   What do you think, girls?

Rachel   Becky, your wish has just come true!

Grammar focus

Present perfect simple with *just, already* and *yet*

Note the position of the words *just, already* and *yet*:

I've **just** seen Eddie.

I've **already** done it.

Have you learnt your lines **yet**?

He hasn't seen it **yet**.

just = a short time ago

already = earlier than expected

yet = up to now

Underline the correct word to complete the rules.

just comes before/after *have*.

already comes before/after *have*.

yet comes at the beginning/end of a sentence.

We usually use *just/already/yet* in questions and negatives.

Comprehension

2 **Choose the correct option:**
Right (✓) Wrong (✗) It doesn't say (?)

1 The pantomime is *Cinderella*.   [✓]

2 Adam practised his lines with his mum.   [ ]

3 Adam is playing the part of an Ugly Sister.   [ ]

4 Eddie's hair is green.   [ ]

5 Eddie's dad thinks the purple wig is great.   [ ]

6 Becky likes the poster.   [ ]

7 Eddie comes to the girls' room to show them his costume.   [ ]

Grammar practice

just/already

3a **Use the prompts to complete the sentences.**

1 Do you want to see the new James Bond film?
No, thanks. (I/already) .... I've already seen .... it.

2 Let's have an ice cream.
No, thanks. (I/just) .... one.

3 You can't go out until you've tidied your room.
(We/already) .... it.

4 What time does the train leave?
Sorry, (it/just) ....

5 Tell Sophie to phone Emma.
(She/already) .... her.

6 What time are Kim and Danny arriving?
(They/just) ....

> Remember you can look up past participles of verbs on page 135.

3b **Put the words in the correct order.**

1 they
Gianni's new
flat Have
yet seen?

Have they seen Gianni's
new flat yet?

2 yet I
finished
haven't

....

3 you
decided
Have
yet?

....
....

4 hasn't
He
yet me
phoned

....
....

5 post the
Has
arrived yet
?

....
....

6 new
We haven't
pool been
yet the to

....
....

Listen

4 **Listen to the conversations. Have these things happened yet?**

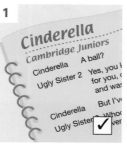

learnt his lines

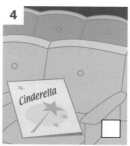

put the programmes on the seats

bought her ticket

heard the orchestra

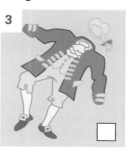

tried on her costume

been on the stage

Extra!

5 **Listen again and look at the chart. Write a sentence about each character.**

1 Adam   4 Becky and Rachel
2 Eddie's gran   5 Rachel
3 Becky   6 Eddie

Adam's already learnt his lines......

Speak

6 **Work with a partner. Think of a new film, CD, or book, or a new place in town.**
Ask and answer using the verbs in the box.

> go   heard   read   see

> A Have you (been to the new shopping centre) yet?

Cinderella

performed by
Cambridge Juniors Football Club

The Cast

Cinderella

Rachel Andrews

Rachel is from Ely. She joined Cambridge Juniors last year and has played in the team for six months. She was born in Scotland but she has lived in Ely since 2001. Rachel is a talented actress. She won the drama prize at school last summer when she starred in the musical *Bugsy Malone*.

Prince Charming

Rebecca Grant

The Ugly Sisters

Edward Green

Eddie has been at Comberton Village College for two years. He has played with Cambridge Juniors for five years. Eddie enjoys being on the stage and making people laugh.

Adam Walker

Adam has been at Parkside School for two years. He has played for Cambridge Juniors since last September and he has been captain for three months. He was in last year's CJFC pantomime. He played the main character, Aladdin. Adam Walker was born in London but has lived in Cambridge for seven years.

Comprehension

7 **Read the programme notes and answer the questions.**

1 Who has lived in another country? ....Rachel...
2 Who has played Aladdin?
3 Who likes comedy?
4 Who has been in a pantomime before?
5 Who has appeared in a musical?
6 Who won a drama prize?

Listen

8 **Listen and complete Becky's details.**

> # Rebecca Grant
> Becky first appeared in a play at the age of ......3..........
> and she's played football since she was ....
> Becky has been captain of her team for .... years.
> and went on tour with her team to Italy in ....

Grammar focus

Present perfect with *for* and *since*

We use ***for*** when we're talking about a period of time:
Adam has been at Parkside School **for** two years.

We use ***since*** when we give the beginning of the time.
He has played for Cambridge Juniors **since** last September.

Find examples of *for* and *since* in the programme notes and write them in the correct columns.

for	since
for 6 months	since 2001

Grammar practice

9 **Complete the sentences with *for* or *since*.**

1 I've been here ...for.... two hours.
2 I been here .... 10 o'clock.
3 He's lived in Moscow .... five years.
4 Adam's mum has worked at the university .... 2002.
5 They haven't seen their cousins .... a long time.
6 She hasn't written to him .... October.

Speak and write

10a **Use the chart to tell your teacher one thing about you, your best friend or your parents.**

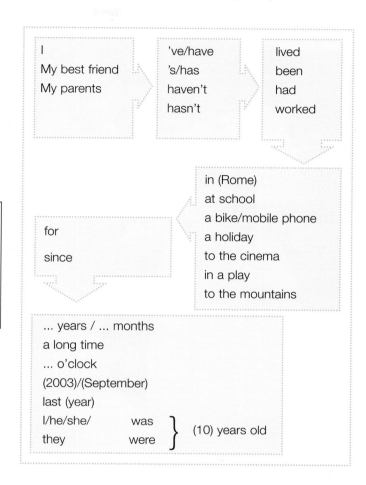

I	've/have	lived
My best friend	's/has	been
My parents	haven't	had
	hasn't	worked

for	in (Rome)
since	at school
	a bike/mobile phone
	a holiday
	to the cinema
	in a play
	to the mountains

... years / ... months
a long time
... o'clock
(2003)/(September)
last (year)
I/he/she/they was/were } (10) years old

10b **Now write five sentences.**

I've been at school since 8 o'clock.
I haven't been in a play since I was five.
My best friend has had a mobile phone for five years.
My parents haven't had a holiday for a long time.

10c **Tell your partner about yourself, your best friend or your parents.**

Extra!

11 **Write a short paragraph about your partner.**

Caterina has lived in Lisbon for twelve years.

🎧 Listen and read

12 **Listen and read.**

Scene 2

Fairy Godmother	What's the matter, Cinderella?
Cinderella	My sisters have gone to the ball. I'm so sad. I wish I could go!
Fairy Godmother	Well, don't worry. Your wish can come true. You can go the ball.
Cinderella	But I haven't got anything to wear!
Fairy Godmother	Here's your dress.
Cinderella	It's lovely!
Fairy Godmother	Just one thing: you must be back by midnight. Good luck!

Scene 3   At the ball

Ugly Sister 2	Look at the Prince. He's so cute!
Ugly Sister 1	But he's been with that girl for ages. He hasn't danced with anyone else all evening.
Ugly Sister 2	Have you danced with anyone yet?
Ugly Sister 1	No. But the Prince will ask me next.
Ugly Sister 2	I don't think so!

Scene 1

Ugly Sister 1	We've just had an invitation to a ball.
Cinderella	A ball?
Ugly Sister 2	Yes, you know, the Prince's ball at the palace. It's not for you, of course. You've got to stay and wash the dishes.
Cinderella	But I've washed the dishes.
Ugly Sister 2	Whoops! Oh dear. My tea has gone all over the floor.
Ugly Sister 1	Never mind, she'll clean it up.
Cinderella	I've already cleaned the floor three times today.
Ugly Sister 2	Let's go and get ready.
Ugly Sister 1	See you later, Cinderella.
Ugly Sister 2	Yes, much later.

Comprehension

13 **Number the sentences in the correct order to summarise the story.**

☐ Cinderella danced all evening with the Prince.

☐ She left her shoe behind and the Prince found it.

☐ At 12 o'clock, Cinderella left the ball quickly.

☐ He went to Cinderella's house. Cinderella tried on the shoe and it fitted.

☐ Cinderella was sad because she was at home alone.

☐ The Fairy Godmother gave Cinderella a beautiful dress and she went to the ball.

[1] The Ugly Sisters received an invitation to the ball at the palace.

Later that evening

Cinderella — Oh, no. The clock has just struck 12. I must go.

Prince Charming — Just a minute! I don't know your name. She's left her shoe! I must find her.

Grammar focus

The Present perfect and the Past simple

We use the **Present perfect** to connect the past with the present:

My sisters have gone to the ball and I'm so sad.

We often use the Present perfect:

- to give news:
  We've just had an invitation to the ball.
- to say how much we've done up to now:
  I've washed the dishes.
- to ask or say if things have happened up to now:
  Have you danced with anyone yet?
- to say how long something has continued up to now:
  He's been with that girl for ages.
- to say how often things have happened up to now:
  I've already cleaned the floor three times today.
- with *just*, *already* and *yet*:
  I've just seen Eddie.

We often use the Past simple:

- to tell a story:
  The Ugly Sisters received an invitation to the ball at the palace.
- to talk about when things happened:
  The Prince had a party last night.

Scene 4

A week has passed since the day of the ball. The prince has looked everywhere for the pretty girl but he hasn't found her yet.

Prince Charming — I'm looking for the owner of this shoe.

Ugly Sister 2 — It's mine.

Ugly Sister 1 — It's not yours. Your feet are much too big. It's mine.

Prince Charming — Perhaps it's yours. What's your name?

Cinderella — Cinderella.

Ugly Sisters — It fits!

Prince Charming — I've found you at last!

Grammar practice

(14) Underline the correct tense.

1 Have you seen/*Did you see* the new *Tintin* film yet?
2 *We have been/We went* to the beach last weekend.
3 Can I go out now? *I've done/I did* all my homework.
4 Italy *have won/won* all their matches so far this season.
5 How many times *have you played/did you play* football this week?
6 They *have arrived/arrived* at 8 o'clock.

Talk time

(15) Listen to these phrases and find them in the play.

1 Never mind	4 much later
2 I wish I could go	5 Just one thing
3 Don't worry	6 for ages

Pronunciation

Stressed syllables

(16) Listen again to Exercise 15. Underline the stressed syllables in the phrases. Practise saying them with a partner.

Speak

(17a) Act out the play.

(17b) Act out one of the scenes from memory.

Portfolio

(18) Record one of the scenes from *Cinderella*. Go to page 129.

Daniel Radcliffe

 Listen and read

1 **Listen and read.**

Who is Daniel Radcliffe?

Daniel Radcliffe was born on 23rd July 1989 and he's already become famous all over the world. Why? Because he is Harry Potter.

When did he become famous?

Daniel was always interested in acting but he never acted in school plays. He auditioned for the part of Harry in July 2000. A few weeks later, the telephone rang.

'My dad picked up the phone in the kitchen,' says Daniel. 'He came upstairs a few minutes later and said, "You've got the part of Harry Potter." I cried. I was so happy.'

Has fame changed him?

Daniel has missed quite a lot of school since he started filming. But he's kept in touch with his school friends. They visited him on the set. Were they jealous?

'No, I don't think so. Everybody has been really nice.'

Like Harry, Daniel is loyal, he's curious and he stands up for himself. He also gets into trouble. His friends are very important to him and this hasn't changed since he became a star.

What does he do in his spare time?

Spare time! He doesn't have much spare time now. But he likes Formula 1 racing and football. He has supported his local team, Fulham Football Club, since he was very young. He likes listening to music, watching *The Simpsons*, keeping fit and being at home with friends. 'We have pizza parties,' says Daniel, 'which means I get some friends round, we eat a pizza, we're really lazy and we play computer games.'

Likes

Books	*The Colour of Magic* by Terry Pratchett
Food	pizza, vanilla ice cream and chocolate sauce
Animals	wolves
Colours	green, red, gold
Number	nine
Hobbies	writing, running, sports, music, reading
School subjects	English
Super hero	Spiderman

Dislikes

School subjects	Maths and French
Food	cake
Jobs at home	making his bed and tidying his room

Comprehension

(2) **Answer the questions and find statements in the text to support your answers.**

1 Did Daniel ever appear on stage at school?
.No,.he.didn't..He.never.acted.in.school.........
.plays...

2 Did Daniel see his school friends during the filming?

3 Is Daniel a good friend?

4 Is Daniel sporty?

5 Is Manchester United Daniel's favourite football team?

 Listen

(3) **Amy and Matthew are talking about Harry Potter. Listen and then answer the questions.**

1 How many *Harry Potter* books has Matthew read?
.He's.read.all.of.them...

2 Which was his favourite?

3 How many times has he read it?

4 Amy has read a *Harry Potter* book recently. How do you know?

5 Which film has Matthew just seen?

6 What's Matthew going to do on Friday evening?

Speak

(4) **Ask and answer with a partner.**

1 Have you ever read a *Harry Potter* book?

2 Which ones have you read? Which did you like best?

3 Which other books have you read recently?

4 Have you ever seen a *Harry Potter* film?

5 Which other films have you seen recently?

6 Have you ever read a book or seen a film more than once?

Write

(5) **Either:**

Write your own chart of likes and dislikes like Daniel's.

Or:

Write three or four sentences about books you've read and films you've seen recently and what you thought about them.

4 Culture spot

School Swap

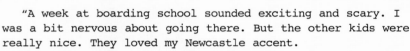

Most children in the UK go to state schools. Secondary schools are usually comprehensive schools. They are open to children of all abilities. State education is free and students don't pay for their books.

Some children go to private schools. They have to pass an entrance exam and their parents have to pay for their education. Many of these schools are boarding schools: students study, eat and sleep there during term-time.

Christopher Willans, 14, usually goes to Kenton Comprehensive School in Newcastle. Fiona Bullen, 14, goes to Dauntsey's, a private boarding school in Wiltshire. Chris and Fiona swapped schools for a week.

"A week at boarding school sounded exciting and scary. I was a bit nervous about going there. But the other kids were really nice. They loved my Newcastle accent.

Dauntsey's is a really old school. It's very strict. When a teacher came into a room, you had to stand up. The work was much harder and the school day was over an hour longer than at home. You also had to do an hour of homework before dinner and another hour afterwards.

At Dauntsey's we slept in 'dorms'. They're big bedrooms for about eight people. It was really good, just like one big sleepover.

I'm sure you get a better education at Dauntsey's but it's more fun at Kenton. You have freedom and TV at the end of the day! Some children have parents with more money, so they can send them to private schools. But the swap taught me that we're all the same really."

Read

1 **Read the text about Chris and Fiona.**

Vocabulary

2 **Find these words in the article and try to guess what they mean from their contexts.**

1 swap (*noun and verb*)
2 accent
3 strict
4 sleepover
5 freedom
6 respect
7 streetwise
8 naive

Comprehension

3 **Which school is it, Dauntsey's (D) or Kenton (K)?**

1 It's a boarding school. ...D...
2 The teachers are strict. ....
3 You don't pay to go there. ....
4 You share a bedroom with several other pupils. ....
5 The classes are big. ....
6 The teachers sometimes have problems with naughty children. ....
7 The school day is longer. ....
8 The school buildings are old. ....
9 You can go out after school. ....
10 You have more homework. ....

"I've been at boarding school since I was nine, so I didn't know what to expect.

I went to stay with a girl called Amanda. She goes to Kenton School. We got on really well. We talked about boys, music, videos and things like that.

The classes at Kenton were big and some of the pupils had no respect for the teachers. They were a lot more streetwise. I felt naive. At Dauntsey's we do homework every night, but when I was staying with Amanda we went swimming, shopping and to the cinema. The freedom was great.

The biggest thing I learnt was that teenagers aren't different just because they go to different kinds of schools."

Speak

(4) **Work with a partner.**
Partner A chooses to be Chris or Fiona.
Partner B asks five questions about Partner A's week at the other school.

Example questions to ask Chris:

What were the other kids like?
What were the teachers like?
Is the school day the same?

Example questions to ask Fiona:

Where did you stay? What was it like?
What was the biggest difference about the school?
What did you do in the evenings?

(5) **Which school would you like best, Kenton or Dauntsey's? Why?**

Write

(6) **Write a paragraph about different kinds of schools in your country. First, answer these questions:**

- How many types of secondary school are there?
- Do you pay to go to any of them?
- Do you pay for your books?
- Do you have to pass an entrance exam?
- Do you stay at school during term-time?
- Are some schools stricter than others?
- What are the good things and bad things about each kind of school?

4

Let's check

Vocabulary check

1 **Match the words to the pictures.**

a

b

c

d

e

f

play   [c]   **3** opera   [ ]
1 musical   [ ]   **4** concert   [ ]
2 comedy   [ ]   **5** ballet   [ ]

Write your score: …/5

2 **Write the words in the gaps.**

| stage | seats | programme |
| costumes | audience | ~~tickets~~ |

I have two .**tickets**. for the play next week. Do you want to come with me?

1 The actors in a play often wear ....
2 The .... loved the play. They laughed at all the jokes and clapped at the end.
3 You can read about the play and the actors in the ....
4 Our .... weren't very good. We couldn't see all the actors on the ....

Write your score: …/5

Grammar check

3 **Correct the mistake in each sentence. ∧ = there's a word missing; X = change one word; ⤷ = change the order of two words; * = you must delete one word.**

She's had that bike for last July. **X**
.She's had that bike since last July......................

1 I'm not watching the video because I seen it already. ∧
....
....
2 I'm free now because I've just done my last exam yet. *
....
....
3 He's been already to Spain and Portugal. ⤷
....
....

4 We've known Max since ten years. **X**
....
5 It's only seven in the morning and Jo's already had breakfast and went to work. **X**
....
....

Write your score: …/5

4 **Choose the correct words for each sentence.**

She has ...**worked**... in that shop for two weeks.
A working   (B worked)   C work
1 She's lived in London … 2001.
A for   B since   C before
2 I've had a mobile phone … a month.
A for   B since   C before
3 I can't lend you any more money. I've … lent you €20
A yet   B already   C been
4 Have you learnt your lines for the play …?
A yet   B just   C ever
5 "Would you like a sandwich?" "No, thanks. … lunch."
A I just had   B I just have   C I've just had
6 We've been friends … primary school.
A for   B since   C until
7 What's the matter? Have you … seen a ghost?
A just   B yet   C later
8 Have you … the History homework yet?
A doing   B done   C did
9 He's only three and he … already learnt to read.
A has   B did   C is
10 Yesterday … for a picnic on the beach.
A we've been   B we were   C we went

Write your score: …/10

5 **Make sentences by putting the words in order.**

an / ice cream / I've / had / never / sandwich
I've never had an ice cream sandwich................

1 brother / a competition / $200 / has / in / just / My / w
....
2 years / in / for / She's / shop / that / worked
....
3 already / holiday / photos / seen / We've / your
....
4 been / doctor / hasn't / see / She / the / to / yet
....
5 been / last birthday / the cinema / hasn't / her / My / mother / since / to
....

Write your score:
Write your total score: .

54

How good are you?

★ I'm not very good at this.   ★★ I'm OK at this.   ★★★ I'm good at this.

Tick (✓) the correct boxes.

		★	★★	★★★

READING I can understand:

a dialogue and e-mail about recent events	*His father's changed jobs and they've moved to Milan. I've been ill this week, so I've been in bed.*			
questions about people's experience	*Have you ever been in a play?*			
a dialogue about how people have prepared for a pantomime	*Have you learnt your lines yet? Let's do the poster. I've already done it.*			
a theatre programme giving biographical details	*She has lived in Ely since 2001.*			
scenes from a pantomime	*Your wish can come true. You can go to the ball.*			
an article about a young film star	*Daniel has missed quite a lot of school since he …*			
an article about children swapping schools	*I'm sure you get a better education at Dauntsey's but it's more fun at Kenton.*			

LISTENING I can understand:

people talking about their experiences and the experiences of others	*I've never climbed a mountain. She's played football since she was five.*			
an interview about a swimming training method	*I've never seen anything so stupid in my whole life.*			
conversations about what has or hasn't already happened	*How's your costume? I've just tried it on.*			
a conversation about books and films	*How many Harry Potter books have you read?*			

WRITING I can write:

about how often people have communicated	*Laura has written a letter to her pen friend in the last week.*			
about how long situations have lasted	*I've been at school since 8.30 this morning.*			
about different kinds of schools in my country	*There are … different types of secondary school.*			

SPEAKING I can:

talk about things I've done this week	*I've played basketball. I've been to the beach.*			
ask and answer questions about how often people have communicated	*In the last week how many text messages have you sent?*			
ask and answer about experiences	*Have you ever climbed a mountain?*			
discuss an unusual swimming training method	*He shouldn't put a crocodile in the pool.*			
talk about how long situations have lasted	*I've lived in Warsaw for a long time.*			
talk about films and books	*Have you ever read a Harry Potter book? Which films have you seen recently?*			

Vocabulary groups

Write three more words in each vocabulary group.

Post office	address	postcode	………………	………………	………………
Communication verbs	post a letter	…………… the net	…………… a message	…………… your e-mails	
Films, shows and plays	comedy	………………	………………	………………	
At the theatre	seat	stage	………………	………………	………………

Module 3

Grammar

If clauses (0 and 1)

If clauses with *may/might*

Making polite requests

Question tags

used to + infinitive

Adjectives followed by
to + infinitive

The infinitive of purpose

Verbs followed by *to* + infinitive

Verbs followed by the *ing* form

Vocabulary

Farms and farm animals

Jobs

Communication

Talking about consequences
and general truths

Talking about possible plans

Making polite requests

Talking about past habitual actions

Giving opinions

Talking about ideal jobs

Pronunciation

Intonation in *if* sentences

Stressed syllables

Culture spot

Homes in Britain

5

Farms and farm animals

1 **Listen and follow.** 🎧

a field
1 sheep
2 bull
3 goat
b cowshed
c farmhouse
d tree
4 rabbit
5 cow
e gate
f barn
6 dog
g farm
7 kittens
h stable
8 fox
9 goose
10 cat
11 horse
i yard
12 donkey
13 hen
j fence
k farmer
14 puppies
15 pig
l pond
16 duck

one goose · two geese
one sheep · two sheep

Do you remember?

in
on
under

behind
in front of
next to

2 **Work with a partner. Ask and answer.**

A Where's the horse?

B It's in the stable.

A Where are the ducks?

B They're on the pond.

5

Saturday morning on the farm

- *If* clauses (0 and 1)
- **Question tags**
- **Talking about consequences and general truths**
- *If* clauses with *may/might*
- **Talking about possible plans**
- **Making polite requests**

🎧 Listen and read

1 Listen and read.

It's Saturday morning. Eddie's got some jobs to do at home.

Mum	Eddie, go and feed the hens and collect the eggs. And then can you sweep the yard?
Eddie	Oh, do I have to?
Mum	Yes, you do. If you don't do your chores, your dad gets cross. And when you've swept the yard, can you wash the car?
Eddie	I'll do it this afternoon.
Mum	If you do it this morning, I'll give you some extra pocket money.
Eddie	OK, I'll do it. Come on, Toby!
Mum	And if you see your dad, tell him to come in for his breakfast. It's bacon and egg.
Eddie	Mmm! If there's any left, I'll have some, too!

Comprehension

2 Which of these jobs is Eddie going to do?

......b.........

a  b

c  d

e  f

Grammar focus

If clauses (0)

You can talk about consequences or general truths by using *if*:
If you don't do your chores, your dad **gets** cross.
If we're late for school, we **get** into trouble.

Use *if* when you're not sure that something is going to happen:
If you see your dad, **tell** him to come in for his breakfast.

Grammar practice

3 Match the two halves of each sentence. ...1 c....

1 If the geese make a noise,
2 If the dog sees a cat,
3 If you buy a sandwich,
4 If you buy one bar of chocolate,
5 If the train is late,
6 If the cows lie down in the field,
7 If you travel after 9.30,

a) he chases it.
b) you can expect rain.
c) it means there are people in the yard.
d) you get a drink free.
e) your ticket is only £2.
f) you get a second bar free
g) we take the bus to school

Grammar focus

If clauses (1)

We can use *if* to talk about events which are likely or possible:

If there's any bacon left, I**'ll have** some, too.

We can also use *if* to bargain and make promises:

If you wash the car this morning, I**'ll give** you some extra pocket money.

Notice that you use the present tense in the *if* clause:
NOT If you ~~will~~ wash the car this morning, I'll give you some extra pocket money.

You can change the order of the clauses, like this:
Tell your dad his breakfast is ready if you see him.
I'll give you some extra pocket money if you wash the car this morning.

Grammar practice

4 **What's Eddie thinking? Write sentences following the pattern.**

(get some extra pocket money)
If I sweep the yard, <u>I'll get some extra pocket money.</u>

(go to the cinema tonight)
<u>If I get some extra pocket money, I'll go to the cinema tonight.</u>

1 (see Becky and Rachel)
<u>If I go to the cinema tonight,</u> ....

....

2 (go for a pizza with them after the film)
<u>If I see Becky and Rachel,</u> ....

....

3 (spend all my money)
If ....

....

4 (not have enough money to go out on Sunday)
If ....

....

5 (have to sweep the yard again)
If ....

....

5 **Put the verbs into the correct tenses.**

1 (be/not have)
You <u>'ll be</u> hungry if you <u>don't have</u> any breakfast.

2 (not leave/not catch)
If he <u>doesn't leave</u> now, he <u>won't catch</u> the train.

3 (come/have)
If you .... to our house on Saturday, we .... a barbecue.

4 (see/tell)
If I .... Mary, I .... her you called.

5 (see/run)
If the fox .... us, it .... away.

6 (take/have)
I .... the dog for a walk if I .... time.

7 (not learn/not listen)
You .... anything if you ....

8 (be/not go)
You .... tired tomorrow if you .... to bed early.

Write

6 **Work with a partner. Write connecting sentences, as in Exercise 4. Start like this:**

If I get up early on Saturday morning, I'll ....

A <u>If I get up early on Saturday morning, I'll clean the kitchen.</u>
B <u>If you clean the kitchen, your mum will give you some money.</u>
A <u>If my mum gives me some money, I'll</u> ....

Pronunciation

Intonation in *if* sentences

7a **Listen. Notice how the tone of the voice goes up at the end of the *if* clause and down at the end of the second clause.**

If I get up early on Saturday morning, I'll clean the kitchen.

7b **Now practise your sentences from Exercise 6 with the correct intonation.**

5

8 **Listen and read.**

Eddie	Come here! It's OK. He won't hurt you.
Dominic	It's all right. I like dogs. What's his name?
Eddie	Toby.
Dominic	Hello, Toby. You're a nice dog, aren't you? My name's Dominic.
Eddie	Hi. My name's Eddie.
Dominic	You live here, don't you?
Eddie	Yes. Where do you live?
Dominic	I live just down the road, in the village.
Eddie	But you're aren't from around here, are you?
Dominic	No, we've just moved here. I'm from Romania.
Eddie	Romania?
Dominic	Yes, my mum's come here to work as a nurse.
Eddie	Which school do you go to? You don't go to Comberton, do you?
Dominic	No, not yet. But I'm starting there next week.
Eddie	Get down, Toby! Don't be a nuisance!
Dominic	It's OK. I love animals!
Eddie	Well, we've got lots. You can come and see them, if you like.
Dominic	Oh, I'd like that! But I'll have to ask my mum first. If it's OK, can I come tomorrow?
Eddie	Yes, fine.

Comprehension

9 **Choose the correct answer.**

1 Dominic
    a) likes animals.
    b) doesn't like animals.

2 Eddie
    a) has met Dominic before.
    b) hasn't met Dominic before.

3 Dominic lives
    a) near Eddie's farm.
    b) a long way from Eddie's farm.
    c) on a farm.

4 Dominic's mum works
    a) in a supermarket.
    b) in a hospital.
    c) on a farm.

5 Dominic
    a) has just started at Comberton School.
    b) has been at Comberton School for a week.
    c) hasn't started at Comberton School yet.

Grammar focus

Question tags

You can use question tags to confirm what you think and to ask for agreement.

Affirmative statement	**Negative question tag**
You're a nice dog,	aren't you?
You live here,	don't you?

Negative statement	**Affirmative question tag**
You aren't from around here,	are you?
You don't go to Comberton School,	do you?

Grammar practice

10 **Write the question tags.**

A

If there is an auxiliary verb (*have, will, be, can, do*), in the statement, use it to make the question tag.
You**'ve** got two brothers, **haven't** you?

She **hasn't** lived here long, **has** she?
We**'ll** see them tomorrow, **won't** we?
It **isn't** snowing yet, **is** it?
We **can** go now, **can't** we?
You **don't** live in Cambridge, **do** you?
They **didn't** go to France, **did** they?

B

If the statement contains the main verb *be,* use it to make the question tag.
You**'re** a nice dog, **aren't** you?
You **aren't** from around here, **are** you?
You **weren't** at school yesterday, **were** you?

C

For all other main verbs, use *do/does* or *did*.
You **live** here, **don't** you?
He **understands** French, **doesn't** he?
They **went** to Italy, **didn't** they?

1 Adam hasn't got any brothers and sisters, ...has he....?
2 Rachel can act and sing, ...?
3 Rachel doesn't go to school in Cambridge, ... ?
4 Eddie doesn't like shopping, ... ?
5 Tommaso hasn't been to a Hallowe'en party, ...?
6 Eddie didn't play the part of Aladdin, ...?

7 Toby is Eddie's dog, ...isn't he........?
8 Dominic's mum is a nurse, ...?
9 Eddie and Adam were the Ugly Sisters in the pantomime, ...?

10 Adam likes reading and listening to music, .doesn't he.?
11 Becky likes volleyball, ...?
12 Eddie enjoys making people laugh, ...?
13 Rachel and Becky had an e-mail from Tommaso, ... ?
14 Adam had a postcard from Eloisa, ... ?

Write

11 **Work with a partner. How much do you know about your partner? Write ten sentences with question tags.**

1 You're (12/sporty/fromBudapest)
   You're 12, aren't you?....?
2 You can (swim/play football)
3 Your birthday's in (January/May)
4 You like (watching TV/reading)
5 You don't like (spiders/snakes)
6 You went to (Florida/the beach) last summer
7 You didn't go to (Paris/Scotland) last year
8 You live in (Coimbra/Oporto)
9 Your favourite colour is (blue/purple)
10 You've got (a hamster/a brother)

Extra!

12 **Check with your partner that what you've written in Exercise 11 is true.**

No, I don't!

You don't like spiders, do you?

5

13 **Listen and read.**

Mum	Come on in, boys, and have some tea and cake.
Dominic	Thank you, Mrs Green. Do you mind if I call my mum? She's expecting me at 5 o'clock.
Mum	No, that's fine. Go ahead. He's very polite, isn't he?
Eddie	So am I.
Mum	Well, sometimes. Would you like a cup of tea, Dominic?
Dominic	Yes, please. But without milk.
Eddie	Ugh! Without milk?
Dominic	Yes, if that's all right.
Mum	Of course it's all right. So did you enjoy yourself this afternoon?
Dominic	Yes, I did. May I come again some time?
Mum	Yes. What about next Sunday afternoon?
Dominic	Oh, I'll have to ask my mum if I can come then. Is it all right if I phone you on Saturday morning?
Eddie	That's OK, isn't it, Mum?
Mum	Yes, that'll be fine. If you come on Sunday you might see some baby lambs.

Comprehension

14 **True or false?**

1 It's lunchtime.
  False.....
2 It's 6 o'clock.
3 Eddie's mum likes Dominic.
4 Dominic likes milk in his tea.
5 Dominic wants to come to the farm again.
6 Dominic is sure he can come next Saturday afternoon.
7 Eddie wants Dominic to come again.

Grammar focus

If clauses + *may/might*

If you come on Saturday, you'll see some baby lambs. (= It's certain.)

If you come on Saturday, you may/might see some baby lambs. (= It's possible.)

You can use either *may* or *might* to talk about a possibility.

May and *might* are the same for all persons of the verb.

62

Grammar practice

15 **Match the two halves and write the complete sentence using *may/might*.**

1g If you don't work hard, you may/might not pass your exams.

1 If you don't work hard,
2 If dad's in a good mood,
3 If you don't want to come to the match,
4 If they go near the bull,
5 If we don't phone Carla to tell her we're late,
6 If we go in for the competition,
7 If we go skiing in early December,

a) he/buy me a CD
b) I/ask Jack to come
c) it/get angry
d) she/not wait for us
e) there/not be any snow
f) we/win
g) you/not pass your exams

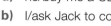

Extra!

16 **Work in groups of four or more. Talk about possible plans for the weekend. Use the picture prompts below to help you.**

If it's sunny at the weekend, …
If it's raining at the weekend, …

A If it's sunny at the weekend, I might go to the beach.

B Oh, that's a good idea. I might come with you./I might do that too.

 Talk time

17a **Listen and complete the dialogues.**

1
A ..Would... you like a cup of tea?
B Yes, ...

2
A Do you mind .... I call my mum?
B Not at all. .... ahead.

3
A .... I come again some time?
B Yes, ... course.

4
A I'll come on Sunday, ... that's all right.
B Yes, that'll .... fine.

5
A Is it all right .... I use the phone?
B Yes, that's fine.

17b **Work with a partner. Invent new sentences using the phrases above.**

A Would you like an apple?

B Yes, please.

Skills development

I love working with animals

I've always loved animals so I volunteered to work at my local animal home. I've worked there for a year and it's just brilliant.

So many animals
I go there every weekend, from nine in the morning until five at night. You have to do a lot of hard work, but you also get really close to the animals. We wash them, brush them, take them for walks, play with them, and generally look after them. There are so many animals. There's a cattery for all the adult cats and there's a kitten room, too. There's also a kennel building. If people find a stray dog, they bring it here. There's a special puppy room for young dogs. The small animals' room is my favourite place. In there we have lots of animals, like rabbits and hamsters. There's a building for boarders, too. People can leave their animals here if they go on holiday. They pay us to look after them.

My own cat and dog home
If you want a pet, you can get one from an animal home. I feel really happy when animals find a proper home, especially when they've been here for months and nobody has been interested in them. If I have enough money one day, I might have my own cat and dog home.

Alice, 14, Wales

 Listen and read

1a Listen and read. Tick (✓) the animals that Alice mentions.

a ✓   b ☐   c ☐   d ☐

e ☐   f ☐   g ☐  h ☐

1b Find a place in the animal home for each of the animals you ticked in 1a. Cat....cattery.

Comprehension

2 Answer the questions.

1 Where is Alice from?
   She's from Wales.......

2 Why does she work at her local animal home?

3 When does she work there?

4 How many different parts of the animal home are there?

5 Apart from cats and dogs, which other animals might you find at the home?

6 What do you call the animals which stay at the home when their owners are on holiday?

7 Why might you go to an animal home?

8 What might Alice do in the future?

Listen

3 Why has each person come to the animal home? Number the pictures in the correct order. Then tick the box to show when they are coming to the home.

a

☐ now
☐ this evening

b
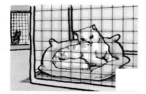
☐ this morning
☐ this afternoon

c

☑ this morning
☐ this afternoon
1

d

☐ at the weekend
☐ next week

e

☐ today
☐ tomorrow

Listen and speak

4a Listen and complete the dialogue.

Daniel is phoning the animal home to ask for a job.

Daniel   Hello, is that the animal home?

Mrs Hall Yes, it ..is....

Daniel   My name's Daniel Smith. Have you .... any jobs at the moment?

Mrs Hall How old are you, Daniel?

Daniel   I'm 14.

Mrs Hall You know we only have volunteers, ... you? We don't pay people to work here.

Daniel   Yes, I know. That's fine.

Mrs Hall Have you .... worked with animals before?

Daniel   No, but I'........ had a cat since I was five and I've looked after my neighbour's dogs when she's been on holiday.

Mrs Hall Can you come on Saturday morning?

Daniel   Well, is it all right .... I come in the afternoon?

Mrs Hall Yes, of .... See you about 2 o'clock?

Daniel   Yes, that's .... Thank you.

4b Role-play the dialogue, changing Daniel's part to fit your own details.

Write

5 Write a letter to the animal home asking for a job.

> • *Write your address here.*
> • *Write the date here.*
>
> Dear Mrs Hall,
>
> I would like to apply for a job at the animal home.
>
> • *Give details of the pets you've had and any other experience with animals.*
> • *Ask if you can come and see her this weekend to talk about a job.*
>
> Yours sincerely
>
> • *Sign your name.*

5

Let's check

Vocabulary check

1 **Match the words to the sentences.**

| hen | pig | donkey | cow | puppy | kitten |

It gives us milk. ....cow............................

1 It gives us eggs. ....
2 It's a baby cat. ....
3 It's a baby dog. ....
4 It's a bit like a horse but it's smaller. ....
5 It gives us bacon, salami and sausages. ....

Write your score: …/5

2 **Match the words to the sentences.**

| farm | field | pond | gate | fence | stable |

Cows eat the grass in it. ....field......................

1 Ducks swim in it. ....
2 You keep horses in it. ....
3 If you don't shut it, the animals will get out. ....
4 The animals here give food – eggs, milk or meat, for example. ....
5 It stops animals getting out of a field. ....

Write your score: …/5

Grammar check

3 **Correct the mistake in each sentence. /\ = there's a word missing; X = change one word; ⤷ = change the order of two words; * = you must delete one word.**

We might to go for a picnic if the weather's nice. *
We might go for a picnic if the weather's nice.

1 If I will see her, I'll give her the message. *
....

2 You'll be late if you won't leave now. X
....

3 If you make a mistake, you always lost one mark. X
....

4 Do you mind I use your telephone? /\
....

5 You didn't eat all the apples, you did? ⤷
....

Write your score: …/5

4 **Circle the correct words for each sentence.**

He hasn't gone to the farm, has he......?
A did he   B was he   C has he *(circled)*

1 If I … your book, I'll send it to you.
A find   B will find   C found

2 If you lend me your camera, I might … the competition.
A winning   B win   C to win

3 You've got green eyes, …?
A haven't you   B aren't they   C aren't you

4 If you know the answer, please … me.
A telling   B told   C tell

5 The film didn't make you laugh, …?
A was it   B did it   C didn't it

6 She's been at the beach all day, …?
A isn't she   B didn't she   C hasn't she

7 Is it all right … I phone you at nine tomorrow?
A for   B when   C if

8 You can't stand on your head, … you?
A do   B are   C can

9 If anybody eats my sweets, … really angry.
A I will   B I was   C I'll be

10 You haven't told my parents, … you?
A did   B have   C were

Write your score: …/10

5 **Write the question tags for these sentences.**

1 You haven't got a dog, ...have you?............
2 You'll send me a postcard from Madrid, ...?
....
3 You broke your tooth in a rugby game, ... ?
....
4 He was playing with the kittens on the farm, ...?
....
5 I don't get angry very often, ...?
6 They won't leave before ten, ...?

Write your score: …/5

Write your total score: …/30

6

Jobs

1 **Match the jobs to the definitions.**

1 ..j......

 1 doctor [j]

 2 actor/ actress [ ]

 3 hairdresser [ ]

 4 farmer [ ]

 5 firefighter [ ]

 **6** zoo-keeper [ ]

 7 photographer [ ]

 8 police officer [ ]

 9 interpreter/ translator [ ]

 **10** TV presenter [ ]

 11 dentist [ ]

 12 scientist [ ]

 13 journalist [ ]

 **14** architect [ ]

a catches criminals
b changes words from one language to another language
c cooks food in a hotel or restaurant
d cuts your hair
e designs houses and other buildings
f does experiments in a laboratory
g fights fires
h helps you in a shop
i introduces TV programmes
j treats you when you're ill
k looks after you on a plane
l looks after your teeth
m looks after animals in a zoo
n performs in a theatre
o plays rock music
p plays sport for money
q rides a horse
r saves people who are in danger in the sea
s shows you interesting places when you're on holiday
t takes photos
u works in a hospital
v works on a farm
w writes for a newspaper or magazine
x looks after animals when they are ill

 15 flight attendant [ ]

 16 sales assistant [ ]

 17 jockey [ ]

 18 chef [ ]

 19 vet [ ]

 20 lifeguard [ ]

 21 nurse [ ]

 22 professional sportsman/ sportswoman [ ]

 23 rock musician [ ]

 24 tourist guide [ ]

2 **Listen and check.** 🎧

🎧 Pronunciation

Stressed syllables

3 **Listen again and underline the stressed syllables in the words in Exercise 1.**

 do<u>c</u>tor

6

It's great to be outside

- *used to* + infinitive
- Talking about past habitual actions
- Adjectives followed by *to* + infinitive
- Giving opinions
- The infinitive of purpose
- Talking about ideal jobs
- Verbs followed by *to* + infinitive
- Verbs followed by the *ing* form

Listen and read

1 **Listen and read.**

Dad	You don't mind getting dirty, do you, Dominic?
Dominic	No, it's great to be outside. I love being with the animals.
Dad	Where do you come from in Romania?
Dominic	Oh, it's just a small village. We used to have a farm. But we had to sell it.
Dad	I'm sorry to hear that.
Eddie	Did you use to help on the farm?
Dominic	Yes, I did. Anyway, my mum decided to apply for a job as a nurse in England.
Dad	And do you like living here?
Dominic	I do now. I didn't want to come at first, though.
Dad	Why was that?
Dominic	It was hard to leave my friends.
Dad	Yes, it isn't easy to make new friends, is it?
Dominic	That's why it was really good to meet Eddie.

Comprehension

2 **Choose the correct option:**
Right (✓) Wrong (✗) It doesn't say (?)

1 Dominic likes being outside. [✓]
2 Eddie's dad has been to Romania. [ ]
3 Dominic lived on a farm in Romania. [ ]
4 Dominic's mum works in a restaurant. [ ]
5 Dominic's happy in England now. [ ]
6 Dominic wants to stay in England. [ ]

Grammar focus

used to
You can use *used to* to talk about past habits and situations.
Affirmative
I **used to** live on a farm.
Negative
I **didn't use to** speak English very well.
Questions and short answers
Did you **use to** have a dog? Yes, I did./No, I didn't.

Grammar practice

3 **Complete the sentence with *used to* and a main verb.**

Affirmative

1 **A:** Have your cousins ever come to see you in Hungary?
   B: Not recently. But they ......used to come......... here every summer.

2 **A:** Have you always had long hair?
   B: No, I .... short hair.

3 He speaks Polish because he .... in Poland.

Negative

4 I like coffee now, but I .... when I was a child.

5 She .... anyone in London, but now she knows lots of people.

Questions

6 We always went to Greece for our holiday when I was younger. Where .... you and your brother ....?

7 **A:** My grandma was a really good singer.
   B: .... she .... opera and that sort of thing?

Speak

4 Work with a partner. Think about when you were five years old. Tell your partner three things about your life then, using *used to*. Your partner must then ask you three questions using *used to*.

> **A** I used to live in a village. I used to have a dog. I used to go to primary school.

> **B** Did you use to play in the garden?

Grammar focus

Adjectives followed by the *to* infinitive
It's great to be outside.

Find the following expressions in the dialogue and complete them.

It isn't easy to ....
It was hard to ....
It was really good to ....
I'm sorry to ....

Grammar practice

5 Write eight sentences that give your opinions.

It's exciting to do wheelies on your bike......

It's dangerous to do wheelies on your bike.

a hard	do wheelies on your bike
b easy	make new friends
c exciting	go to other countries
d great	eat too much chocolate
e silly	spend all your pocket money at once
f interesting	learn a new language
g nice	drive fast
h important	run a kilometre in 3 minutes
i dangerous	
j impossible	

Listen

 Listen

6 Listen to Amy (A) and Ben (B) giving their opinions about the activities below. Write the letter of the correct adjective from Exercise 5 for each of them.

1 A [i] B [c]   5 A [ ] B [ ]
2 A [ ] B [ ]   6 A [ ] B [ ]
3 A [ ] B [ ]   7 A [ ] B [ ]
4 A [ ] B [ ]   8 A [ ] B [ ]

1

2

3

4

5

6
Guten Tag!

7

8
1KM

Extra!

7 Compare your opinions with your partner's. How many are the same?

> **A** I think it's exciting to do wheelies on your bike.

> **B** So do I./I think it's dangerous.

6

Listen and read

8 Listen and read. Whose diary is this?

Saturday
I went into town to buy some things for school. I met Eddie.

Sunday
I went to Eddie's farm to help with the horses.

Monday
I got up early to go to school. My first day! Mum took me to the bus stop to catch the bus.

Tuesday
I stayed up late to finish my homework. It's hard to write in English! Tomorrow I'm going to the football club to meet Eddie's friends.

Comprehension

9 Put the pictures in the order of events.

Grammar practice

10 Work with a partner. Ask your partner these questions. Your partner must answer without looking at Dominic's diary.

1 Why did Dominic go into town?
   He went into town to buy some things for school./To buy some things for school.
2 Why did Dominic go to Eddie's farm?
3 Why did he get up early on Monday?
4 Why did his mum take him to the bus stop?
5 Why did he stay up late on Tuesday night?
6 Why is he going to the football club tomorrow?

Grammar focus

The infinitive of purpose
I went into town **to buy** some things for school.
I went to Eddie's farm **to help** with the horses.
You can use *to* with the infinitive to say why someone does something.

11 Rewrite these sentences using an infinitive with *to*.

1 I'm staying in tonight. I want to watch Episode 1 of *Star Wars*.
   I'm staying in tonight to watch Episode 1 of *Star Wars*.
2 I'm going to wash the car because I need to earn some pocket money.
3 He ran to the station. He wanted to catch the early train.
4 We went to Richard's house. We wanted to revise for our exams.
5 He dialled 999. He asked for an ambulance.
6 Use my computer if you want to send an e-mail.

12 Write your own diary for three days last week. You can use the phrases in the box to help you.

I went	into town	to buy
	to the cinema	to see
	to the park	to meet
	to the shopping centre	to play
		to watch
I stayed at home		to do
I stayed up late		to go
I got up early		

 Read and listen

13a Read and complete the dialogue.

Eddie	I've brought a friend along. Is it ..all...... right if he joins in?
Mike	Yes, ... fine. What's your ....?
Dominic	Dominic.
Mike	Nice to meet you Dominic. I'm Mike.
Dominic	Nice to meet you, too.
Mike	.... on. Let's get started.

After the training session

Rachel	Hi. I'm Rachel and this .... Becky.
Becky	Hi Dominic. How did it go?
Dominic	It was great. I really enjoyed ....
Becky	Well, ... you next week then.
Dominic	Yes, OK.

13b Listen and check.

Talk time

14a Write the correct phrases in the speech bubbles.

I didn't want to come at first
How did it go?
~~I've brought a friend along.~~
Let's get started.
Nice to meet you.
Nice to meet you, too.

1 I've brought a friend along.

2

3

4 ...., but I really enjoyed it.

14b You've taken your English pen-friend to play volleyball with some friends. Write a dialogue using the phrases in Exercises 13a and 14a.

You:	Hi. I've brought a friend along.
Friend 1:	....
William:	....
You:	....

At home, your mum/dad asks William about the match:

| Mum/Dad: | How...? |
| William: | .... |

6

What's your ideal job?
Try this quiz and find out

	Yes	No
1 Do you want to earn a lot of money?		
2 Do you like working late?		
3 Do you enjoy being the centre of attention?		
4 Do you hope to be famous one day?		
5 Do you hate wearing smart clothes?		
6 Do you fancy working with animals?		
7 Do you enjoy working on your own?		
8 'I love being outside.' Is this true for you?		
9 Have you ever tried to design your ideal house?		
10 Do you plan to go to college/university?		
11 Do you enjoy cooking/drawing/taking photos/making things?		
12 'I never give up working on a problem until I've found the answer.' Is this true for you?		
13 Do you enjoy solving problems?		
14 Do you like doing scientific experiments?		
15 When you start doing something, do you always finish doing it?		
16 Do you prefer working inside?		
17 Do you need to do sport more than once a week?		
18 Would you like to be part of a team?		
19 Do you enjoy training and keeping fit?		
20 'I don't mind doing difficult or dangerous things.' Is this true for you?		
21 Do you expect to travel in your job?		
22 Have you learnt to speak any foreign languages?		
23 When you meet someone, do you start to talk to them immediately?		
24 'I can't help wanting to find out about other people.' Is this true for you?		

72

Key

actor/actress	singer	rock musician	TV presenter
farmer	zoo-keeper	vet	jockey
designer	architect	chef	photographer
scientist	doctor	nurse	dentist
professional sportsman/ sportswoman	firefighter	police officer	lifeguard
journalist	flight attendant	tourist guide	interpreter/ translator

Grammar focus

Verb + *to* + infinitive
Some verbs are followed by *to* + infinitive:
I want **to be** an airline pilot.
We need **to buy** a present for Silvia.

Verb + *ing* form:
Other verbs are followed by the *ing* form:
I **enjoy going** to the cinema.
I've **given up playing** the piano.

Put the verbs from the quiz into the correct column.

Verbs followed by *to* + infinitive	Verbs followed by the *ing* form
want	enjoy

These verbs can either be followed by *to* + infinitive or by the *-ing* form:

I love/like/don't like/prefer/hate **to be** outside.
I love/like/don't like/prefer/hate **being** outside.

But notice that *would like* must be followed by *to* + infinitive:

I would like **to go** to the cinema tomorrow.

Read and speak

15 **Work with a partner. Ask and answer the questions in the quiz. Note down your partner's answers.**

Which colour is the section which has the most 'Yes' answers? Find that colour in the key on the left and ask your partner to choose one of the jobs, like this:

> **A** Would you like to be an actor, a singer, a rock musician or a TV presenter?

> **B** I'd like to be a singer.

Grammar practice

16 **Write eight sentences that are true for you. You can add information if you like.**

I enjoy travelling to other countries.
I would like to be a rock star.

want hope plan would like	+ to	go to university be famous do an interesting job go out with friends have my hair cut
enjoy don't mind	+ ing	be (famous) make new friends take photos
like love hate don't like	+ to/ ing	travel do the washing up speak English get up early/late watch sport on TV stay at home at the weekend swim in the sea

Speak

17 **Work with a partner. Partner A: Read your sentences from Exercises 16 to Partner B. Partner B: Tell your teacher as many things as you can remember about Partner A.**

> **B** Enrique likes watching football on TV. He wants to be a famous footballer.

Portfolio

18 **Write a profile of the people in your family and the jobs they do. Go to page 130.**

Skills development

The teenagers

We talked to six American teenagers about their lives. These are the questions we asked:

1 Where do you live?
2 What are you into?
3 How's school?
4 What's the most important thing to you?
5 What are your hopes for the future?

Meredith, 13

1 Ann Arbor, Michigan. I live in the suburbs. There's nothing to do there.
2 I like shopping and going ice-skating or swimming with my friends. I read tons of magazines, and I love Latin Music.
3 I go to a coed* private school. I enjoy it. It's very competitive, but the teachers are friendly.
4 Getting good grades at school, weekends, my cat and dog.
5 I want to go to college* and then maybe work in fashion.

Emma, 16

1 Near Augusta, Maine. It's small, scenic, and quiet.
2 Music is my passion (guitar and saxophone). I'm into R'n'B, rock, classical, and jazz. I also love e-mail and the internet.
3 Great! I go to a small public school*. I'm into geography and maths.
4 My computer, so I can surf and e-mail friends. My piano – music is like breathing to me.
5 I want a good career like my mom. I want to do well and go to Harvard or Yale.

Dave, 16

1 Austin, Texas. It's fantastic. There are tons of shops, movie theaters*, and coffee houses*.
2 Music, especially country and western. I like judo, and I go to the gym as well. I also do some volunteer work.
3 I go to a huge public school. I like it there.
4 Freedom to choose what I want to do.
5 I want to go to college, and I want to be an engineer.

Karl, 14

1 Tacoma, Washington. It's kind of a dump, but it's small and friendly. It's near Seattle.
2 I'm into art, movies, and the theater. I spend a lot of time talking with my friends.
3 I go to a large public school. It's fairly strict, but it's okay. My best subject is art.
4 Everything is important to me: friends, family, and my independence.
5 I want to go to college to study art. I'd love to live in Paris.

Kristin, 14

1 Atlanta, Georgia. The shopping is awesome*, and there are tons of under-21 nights at the clubs.
2 I go to drama classes every Saturday. I love pop music, shopping, and watching sitcoms*.
3 I go to an all-girls' private school. It's friendly, and the teachers are fun, but I really hate exams.
4 Friends, family, the environment, achieving my goals, chocolate.
5 I want to be a TV announcer. I'd like to take a year out to travel and to learn a language.

Shane, 13

1 Greeley, Colorado. It's okay. I spend most weekends with my family at our cabin* in Boulder.
2 Snowboarding. I also like basketball and soccer* and hanging out with my buddies in the mountains. I work for extra money – that teaches me about life.
3 It's a college prep school. It's a good school. I'm mainly into sports.
4 Mom and Dad. You only get one set of parents!
5 I just want to ski or snowboard. I'd like to travel and maybe live in Switzerland for a while.

*a coed school has both boys and girls.
*college = university
*a public school = a state school
*a movie theater = cinema
*coffee houses = cafés

*awesome = wonderful
*sitcoms = soap operas
*cabin = a small wooden house in the forest or mountains
*soccer = football

Read

1 Read the article and look at the photo. Can you guess who's who?

Vocabulary

2 Circle the correct meaning.

1 What are you into?
 a) What are you doing?
 b) What do you like doing?

2 I read tons of magazines.
 a) I read lots of magazines.
 b) I don't often read magazines.

3 It's scenic.
 a) It's not a very nice place.
 b) It's a beautiful place.

4 I want a good career.
 a) I want a big car.
 b) I want a good job.

5 It's kind of a dump.
 a) It's not a very nice place.
 b) It's a beautiful place.

6 drama classes
 a) classes that prepare you for college
 b) acting classes

7 a college prep school
 a) a public high school for boys and girls
 b) a school that helps you get ready for college

8 hanging out with my buddies
 a) talking on the phone to my friends
 b) spending time with my friends

Comprehension

3 Answer the questions.

1 Who's good at painting and drawing? .Karl.....
2 Who likes animals?
3 Who likes acting?
4 Who likes computers?
5 Who wants a job in television?
6 Who likes being near the mountains?
7 Who plays a musical instrument?
8 Who goes to a school where there are no boys?
9 Which two people work?
10 Which two people would like to live in another country?

Listen

4 Who's talking? 1 Emma..........

Speak

5 Work with a partner. Ask and answer the questions from the magazine article.

A Where do you live?

B I live in Castello. It's a small town, but I like it.

Write

6 Write a profile of yourself, answering the questions, like the profiles in the magazine article.

Tacoma
Augusta
Ann Arbor
Greely
Atlanta
Austin

Culture spot

Homes in Britain

> Hi! I'm Kim. I live in a block of flats called Morley House. It's close to the city centre. Our flat is on the seventh floor. It's nice to look out over the city.

> I'm Bradley James. I live in a terraced house in Hill Road. On my side of the street, the numbers are all even: 2, 4, 6, 8 and so on. On the other side, the numbers are all odd: 1, 3, 5, 7 and so on. It's a very friendly street. Everyone knows each other.

> Hi! I'm Charlene. I live in Twickenham. Our house is detac... and it's got four bedrooms. It's a funny house, because it looks o... but actually it's quite new. It's ca... Richmond House. We've lived h... since 1998.

🎧 Listen and read

1 **Listen and read.**

Vocabulary

2 **How many types of home are mentioned? Which are similar to homes in your country?**

Comprehension

3 **Complete the questions with the correct question word and write the answers.**

Where	What	Who	Which

1 ..What.. does Claudia want?
..She wants a normal house....

2 .... lives in a house with an even number?

3 .... lives on a houseboat?

4 .... floor does Kim live on?

5 .... does Charlene live?

6 .... do the signs on Jack's estate say?

Hello. I'm Claudia. We used to live in a caravan. Now we live in a houseboat on a canal. It's a bit small but it's bigger than the caravan! My dad's an artist, and he likes it, but my brother and I want a normal house like everybody else!

Hello. I'm Jack. I live in a semi-detached house on a housing estate just outside York. I quite like it here, but there's nowhere to play football. Everywhere there are signs saying 'No Ball Games'. I think that's a bit unfair.

 Listen

4 **Listen to these people. What sort of accommodation do they want?**

a) a flat in London
b) a farm
c) a houseboat
d) a large detached family house
e) a terraced house in a friendly street

1 Aisha ....e) a terraced house............
2 Andy ....
3 Penny ....
4 Stuart ....
5 Ali ....

Write

5 **Write a description of where you live, as in Exercise 1.**

Speak

6 **Read your description out to the class. The class can ask you questions to find out more information. Answer their questions.**

Example questions
- How long have you lived there?
- Is it close to the city centre?
- Is it old or new?
- What can you see from the windows?
- Is there anywhere to play football?
- Do your grandparents live near you?

Let's check

Vocabulary check

1 **Who is speaking? Write the correct job in each gap.**

interpreter	flight attendant	architect
journalist	lifeguard	~~nurse~~

'I'm working with sick children at the moment.' ....nurse....

1 'At the moment I'm designing a sports centre.'
....

2 'I'm interviewing an actor today. I work for a newspaper.'
....

3 'To do my job you have to be a good swimmer.'
....

4 'I like travelling but I don't like my uniform.'
....

5 'Sometimes you can't think of the right words but you have to say something anyway.' ....

Write your score: ..../5

2 **Choose the correct word to answer each question.**

chef	~~dentist~~	hairdresser
sales assistant	tourist guide	vet

Who looks after your teeth? ..A dentist...

1 Who cuts and washes your hair? ....

2 Who helps you in shops? ....

3 Who cooks food in a restaurant? ....

4 Who looks after animals when they're ill? ....

5 Who shows you interesting places when you're on holiday? ....

Write your score: ..../5

Grammar check

3 **Correct the mistake in each sentence.**

/\ = there's a word missing; X = change one word; ⤷ = change the order of two words; * = you must delete one word.

I stayed up late for to see a film on TV last night. *
I stayed up late to see a film on TV last night...

1 It isn't easy be on stage in front of your friends. /\
....

2 We haven't use to have sheep on this farm. X
....

3 Where you did use to live? ⤷
....

4 My father use to ride a motorbike but he sold it. X
....

5 We went to the market for to buy some fruit. *
....

Write your score: ..../5

4 **Circle the correct words for each sentence.**

I _used to_ live near the river.
A use to   B used to   C used

1 I was sorry … about your problem.
A hearing   B heard   C to hear

2 She hates … up early.
A for getting   B getting   C get

3 We used to … in a small village.
A live   B living   C lived

4 I stayed up late … my mum's friend on TV.
A to see   B for see   C for seeing

5 It's really difficult … a horse with your eyes shut.
A ride   B for ride   C to ride

6 Did you enjoy … that dance in the school play?
A doing   B do   C to do

7 I got up early this morning … my Science.
A for finish   B for finishing   C to finish

8 Have you finished … that picture of Carmen?
A drawing   B to draw   C draw

9 Miguel is learning … the electric guitar.
A play   B playing   C to play

10 Did you … to have sheep on your farm?
A use   B used   C using

Write your score: .../10

5 **Make sentences by putting the words in order.**

a job / apply / for / as a / decided / I've / to / tourist guide
I've decided to apply for a job as a tourist guide.

1 didn't / hair / have / red / She / to / use /
....

2 after / doing / mind / I don't / the washing-up / dinner
....

3 and I / Juan / go / the / same / to / school / to / used
....

4 club / decided / join / has / My / photography / sister / the / to
....

5 all / on sweets / It's / money / pocket / silly / spend / to / your
....

Write your score: ..../

Write your total score: ..../3

How good are you?

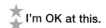

★ I'm not very good at this.   ★/★ I'm OK at this.   ★/★/★ I'm good at this.

Tick (✓) the correct boxes.

		★	★/★	★/★/★
READING I can understand:				
a dialogue about family chores	*If you do it this morning, I'll give you some extra pocket money.*			
a dialogue between people getting to know each other	*You live here, don't you? But you aren't from around here, are you?*			
an article about a volunteer at an animal home	*People can leave their animals here if they go on holiday.*			
a conversation about a lifestyle that has ended	*We used to have a farm but we had to sell it.*			
a quiz about an ideal job	*Do you enjoy working on your own? Have you ever tried to design your ideal house?*			
an article about teenagers' views on life	*I'm into art, movies, and the theater.*			
an article about homes in Britain	*We used to live in a caravan. Now we live in a houseboat on a canal.*			
LISTENING I can understand:				
phone conversations to an animal home	*There's a dog in my garden. It's been there for ages.*			
people giving their opinions on various activities	*I think it's silly to eat too much chocolate.*			
who people are from their views and interests	*The Art teacher's taking us on an Art trip to Paris. I've always wanted to go to Paris. Can I go?*			
people talking about places to live	*We want to live in the country.*			
WRITING I can write:				
a letter applying to be a volunteer at an animal home	*I would like to apply for a job at the cat and dog home.*			
my opinions on various activities	*It's dangerous to drive fast. It's hard to make new friends.*			
a diary for three days last week	*I went to the park to meet my friends.*			
a conversation introducing people	*Hi, I've brought a friend along.*			
a profile of myself	*I'm into music and art. I'm not very interested in sport.*			
a description of where I live	*We live in a flat in the centre of Lisbon.*			
SPEAKING I can:				
talk about possible plans for the weekend	*If it's sunny, we can go for a bike ride.*			
role-play a job interview	*Have you ever worked with animals before?*			
tell the class about my partner's likes and dislikes, hopes and plans	*Matteo would like to be a famous footballer. He doesn't mind getting up early.*			

Vocabulary groups

Write three more words in each vocabulary group.

Farm animals	cow	horse	....	....	....
Places/Things on a farm	field	gate	....	....	....
Jobs	doctor	farmer	....	....	....

Grammar

Relative pronouns: *who, which/that, where, whose*

The Present simple passive

Pronouns and adverbs beginning *some-, any-, every-, no-*

Reported commands

If clauses (2)

Vocabulary

House contents

Illness and injury

Communication

Booking accommodation

Talking about what might happen and about imaginary situations in the future.

Pronunciation

The sound /ʃ/

The letters *gh*

Culture spot

Scotland, Wales and Ireland

7

House contents

1 Listen to the description of the kitchen and living area of this house.
Find the items mentioned and tick (✓) the boxes.

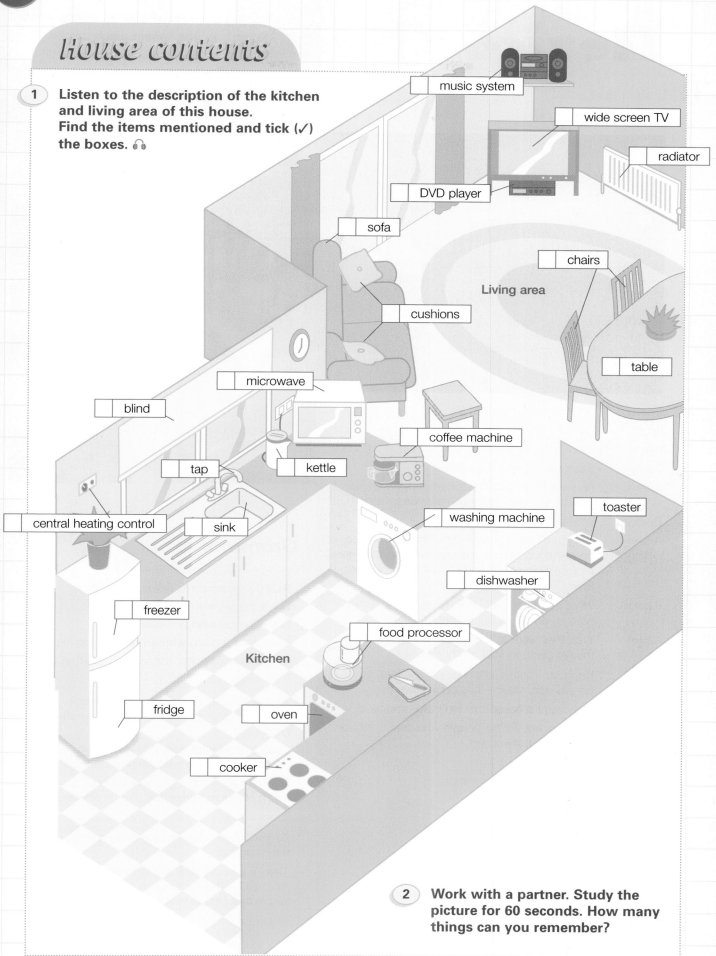

music system

wide screen TV

radiator

DVD player

sofa

chairs

Living area

cushions

table

microwave

blind

coffee machine

tap

kettle

toaster

central heating control

sink

washing machine

freezer

dishwasher

food processor

fridge

oven

Kitchen

cooker

2 Work with a partner. Study the picture for 60 seconds. How many things can you remember?

7

The girl who lives in
Mexico City

- Relative pronouns:
  who, which/that, whose, where
- The Present simple passive
- Booking accommodation

🎧 Listen and read

1 **Listen and read.**

Adam	I've had an e-mail from Eloisa.
Eddie	Eloisa?
Becky	You know, she's the girl who lives in Mexico City.
Rachel	She's the girl who Adam likes.
Adam	Anyway, she's coming to Cambridge with her parents and they need somewhere to stay.
Becky	Why are they coming here?
Adam	Her mum's an archaeologist. She's coming to do some research at the university, so they need a place which isn't too far from the centre of town.
Rachel	What sort of place? Do they want to stay in a hotel or do they want to rent a house?
Adam	Well, they want to find somewhere to rent but they're going to stay in a hotel first.
Eddie	Hang on! There's a house near the farm which people rent. Maybe they could have that.
Adam	They want a house that isn't too expensive.
Eddie	My mum knows the people who own it. I'll ask her to give them a ring.

Comprehension

2 **Answer the questions.**

1 Who has written to Adam? ...Eloisa....
2 Where does Eloisa live?
3 Why has she written to Adam?
4 What is Eloisa's mum going to do in Cambridge?
5 Where are Eloisa's family going to stay when they first arrive?
6 Where is there a house to rent?

Grammar focus

Relative pronouns: *who, which, that*

She's the girl **who** lives in Mexico City.

She's the girl **who** Adam likes.

They want a place **which/that** isn't too expensive.

There's a house near the farm **which/that** people rent.

To give specific information about people, use *who* and remember to take out the personal pronoun.

She's the girl **who** lives in Mexico City.
(NOT: She's the girl who ~~she~~ lives in Mexico City.)

My mum knows the people **who** own it.
(NOT: My mum knows the people who ~~they~~ own it.)

To give specific information about things, use *which* or *that*.

There's a house near the farm **which/that** people rent. (NOT: There's a house near the farm which/that people rent ~~it~~.)

Grammar practice

3 **Complete the sentences with *who* or *which/that*.**

1 What's the name of the boy .....*who*........ plays Harry Potter?

2 I've got a coin ....*which*....... is a hundred years old.

3 I saw the car .... they used in the *Harry Potter* film.

4 He's got an uncle .... works in Hollywood.

5 Do you know a restaurant .... is open on Sunday evenings?

6 Who was the girl .... played Cinderella in the pantomime?

7 We were in the team .... went to Italy.

8 They're the people .... own the house near the farm.

4 **Join the sentences with *who* or *which/that*.**

1 That's the dog. It chased me while I was running in the park.
   <u>That's the dog which chased me while I was</u>
   <u>running in the park.</u>

2 This is my cousin. My cousin comes from California.
   <u>This is my cousin who comes from California.</u>

3 Can I borrow the Blue CD? You bought the Blue CD at the weekend.

4 Have you got a pen? Can I borrow it?

5 She's the girl from Ireland. She's in a band.

6 What's the name of the actor? He played 007 in the last Bond film.

7 Lance Armstrong is an American cyclist. He's won the Tour de France five times.

8 Becky liked the poster. Rachel did the poster.

Speak and write

5a **Work with a partner. Take turns to identify the people and things in the photos. You can use the clues to help you. But be careful, the clues are in the wrong order.**

Clues

a Cinderella lost it at the ball.
b Rachel bought it in Verona.
c Tommaso wore it in the football tournament.
d Eddie bought them in Verona.
e Eddie met him in the field.
f He danced with Cinderella.
g They were horrible to Cinderella.

> This is the poster which Rachel bought in Verona.

0 poster

1 shoe

2 the number 8 shirt

3 chocolates

4 boy

5 sisters

6 prince

5b **Write the captions.**

6 **Listen and read.**

Agent This is the kitchen. It's got a cooker, a fridge, a freezer and a washing machine. There's gas central heating.

Becky Look, it's got a dishwasher. And it makes a lovely noise!

Rachel Is there a microwave?

Agent No, I'm afraid there isn't. And this is the family room. It's got a wide screen TV and a music system.

Becky Is there a DVD player?

Agent No, but there's a video player. The wood for the fire is stored in the shed. The rubbish bins are kept in the garage and the rubbish is collected once a week. There's a lady who comes in to clean. Her name's Mrs Jones. And the grass is cut once a week by her husband.

Mum Is the house available from the beginning of June?

Agent I'm afraid not. It's available from the middle of June. And, by the way, dogs are not allowed, because of the sheep on the farm.

Eddie It's much better than our house. Can we move in, Mum?

Comprehension

7 **Tick (✓) the items that are in the house.**

INVENTORY	
Kitchen	**Family room**
cooker ✓	TV
microwave	DVD player
fridge	music system
freezer	video player
washing machine	
dishwasher	

Grammar focus

Present simple passive
Mr Jones **cuts** the grass.
Cuts is an active verb.
The grass **is cut** by Mr Jones.
Is cut is a passive verb.

To make the passive, use the Present simple of **be** + the **past participle**:
is + cut
We often use the passive to talk about formal arrangements and rules:
Breakfast **is served** at 8.30.
Dogs **are not allowed**.

We also use the passive when it's not relevant to specify a particular person or when we don't know who the person is:
The wood **is stored** in the shed.
The rubbish bins **are kept** in the garage.
If we want to specify a person we use *by*:
The grass **is cut by** Mr Jones.

Remember there is a list of past participles on page 135.

Grammar practice

8a **Make these active sentences passive.**

1 We grow olives in southern Spain.
   <u>Olives are grown in southern Spain.</u>
2 They make paper from trees.
3 They collect the rubbish on Tuesday.
4 We keep the bikes in the garage.
5 We teach French, Spanish and Italian at this school.
6 They don't allow traffic here.
7 They don't allow smoking in the theatre.
8 Which languages do people speak in Canada?

8b **Complete these signs, notices and invitations.**

accept

1 Traveller's cheques <u>are accepted</u>. here.

not allow

2 Dogs ....
  .... on the grass.

speak

3 English and French
  ....
  here.

deliver

4 All pizzas
  ....
  free of charge.

invite

5 You
  ....
  to a Grand Ball at the
  Palace.

Grand Invitation to the Palace Ball

not serve

6 Alcohol
  ....
  to under-18s.

Talk time

9 **Complete the dialogue with the phrases in the box. Then listen and check.**

| by the way | I'm afraid | maybe |
| Hang on | I'm afraid not. | ~~What sort of?~~ |

Assistant	Hello. Can I help you?
Customer	I'm going to a fancy dress party on Saturday and I'd like to hire a costume.
Assistant	<u>What sort of</u>........ costume?
Customer	It's got to be an animal costume, so .... a gorilla.
Assistant	No, I'm sorry, ... I haven't got any gorillas.
Customer	Well, have you got a bear costume?
Assistant	....
Customer	Oh.
Assistant	...................................! I've got a mouse costume. Here it is.
Customer	That's perfect. I'll take it.
Assistant	Oh, ..., be careful at the party.
Customer	Why?
Assistant	I've just hired out two cat costumes.

Extra!

10 **Work with a partner. Act out the dialogue in Exercise 9 from memory.**

Listen and read

11 **Listen and read.**

Adam	Hi, Mum! We've found a house where Eloisa can stay.
Mum	Eloisa?
Adam	You know, the girl whose mother's an archaeologist.
Mum	Oh, that's nice. I'm looking forward to meeting her.

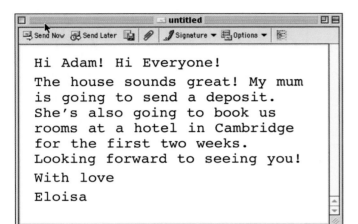

Hi Adam! Hi Everyone!
The house sounds great! My mum is going to send a deposit. She's also going to book us rooms at a hotel in Cambridge for the first two weeks.
Looking forward to seeing you!
With love
Eloisa

Calle San Juan, 17
Colonia Hidalgo
México 22 DF
México
April 15th

Dear Sir or Madam,

I would like to book two rooms for two weeks, starting on June 1st. I'd like a double room and a single room with ensuite bathrooms. Could you tell me how much the rooms will cost per night, and if breakfast is included?

Yours faithfully

Lidia Guzmán

Lidia Guzmán (Mrs)

Comprehension

12 **Answer the questions.**

1 What is Eloisa's mother's job?
.She's an archaeologist.....

2 What does Eloisa think of the house which Eddie and his friends saw?

3 Where are Eloisa and her parents going to stay at first?

4 How long are they going to stay there?

5 When are they arriving?

6 How many rooms do they want?

Grammar focus

Relative pronouns: *whose* **and** *where*

Whose gives information about the relationship between people (and things):

You know, the girl **whose** mother's an archaeologist.

Where gives specific information about places:
We've found a house **where** Eloisa can stay.

Grammar practice

13 **Complete the sentences with** *who,* *which/that, where* **or** *whose*.

1 This is the hotel ....where...... Eloisa and her family are going to stay.

2 Is Dominic the boy .... mother is a nurse?

3 That's the photographer .... we met at the airport.

4 Becky's mum loved the perfume .... Becky bought in Italy.

5 Do you remember the café .... we had hot chocolate with Tommaso?

6 Where are the biscuits .... you bought?

7 Did Adam get the e-mail .... Eloisa sent?

8 We spoke to the woman .... looks after the house.

9 Is that the boy .... parents are farmers?

10 Let's find a place .... we can sit down.

Listen

14a Listen to the conversation between Mrs Guzmán and the receptionist at The Red Lion Hotel. On the chart, tick (✓):

- the kind of accommodation that Mrs Guzmán wants
- the cost per night
- the facilities that The Red Lion has

The Red Lion Hotel

	The Red Lion Hotel	The Regent Hotel	The Ship Inn
Accommodation			
single room	✓ £55		
double room	✓ £		
twin-bedded room			
breakfast			
Facilities			
bathroom ensuite			
shower ensuite			
restaurant			
parking			
satellite TV			
telephone			
indoor pool			
gym			
air conditioning			
kettle/coffee maker			
fridge/mini bar			
internet access			

14b Now listen to these two conversations and complete the chart for The Regent Hotel and The Ship Inn.

 Pronunciation

The sound /ʃ/

15 Listen to the sound /ʃ/ in these words. Can you add any words to the list?

1	accommodation	4	invitation
2	air conditioning	5	conversation
3	receptionist	6	communication

Write

16 Imagine you're going to England with your family. Write a letter to a hotel to ask about accommodation. Use Mrs Guzmán's letter as a model.

Speak

17 Now imagine you want to make the booking by telephone. Work in pairs, taking it in turns to play the receptionist and the guest.

Guest	I'd like to book .... rooms for two nights please, April 25th and 26th.
Receptionist	Yes, of course. What sort of rooms do you need?
Guest	I'd like ...., please.
Receptionist	Would you prefer rooms with showers or bathrooms ensuite?
Guest	..............................., please.
Receptionist	OK. That's fine.
Guest	How much ....?
Receptionist	.... per night.
Guest	Is that for the room or per person?
Receptionist	It's for the room.
Guest	And is breakfast included?
Receptionist	Yes, it is.

 Extra!

18 Continue the conversation. Ask about the facilities at the hotel.

Skills development

The holiday of a lifetime

The beds are covered with reindeer skins

Inside the Ice Hotel

The Jukkasjärvi Ice Hotel

Location
Lapland, 125 kilometres north of the Arctic Circle.

Landscape
Crystal blue lakes, mountains, glaciers, waterfalls, fast rivers and vast forests.

The hotel
The Ice Hotel is open from December to April. It is made from 30,000 tonnes of snow and 1200 tonnes of ice which is cut from the Torne River. It is rebuilt every winter. It takes six to eight weeks to complete. Then in May, it is demolished.

Staying at the hotel
The Ice Hotel is the most unusual hotel you'll ever stay in. It can accommodate a hundred people. Everything is made from ice, including the coffee tables, chandeliers, glasses and even the beds. Guests are given cold-weather suits and sleeping bags. The beds are covered with reindeer skins to keep you warm at night. There's no heating in the hotel. Inside, the temperature is always between -5° and -7 °C. But The Ice Hotel is very popular and there's lots to do. For example, you can go snowmobiling, skiing and dog sledding – all in the same day!

El Hotelito Desconocido – 'The little hotel which nobody knows about'

Location	Near Puerto Vallarta, Mexico.
Landscape	The hotel is on the beach, beside the Pacific Ocean. It is a tropical paradise, surrounded by coconut palms.
The hotel	The hotel is not one big building. It's a series of cottages which are built on stilts along a lagoon, next to the beach. Each cottage has an outdoor bath and shower which overlook the Pacific Ocean. The hotel is solar-powered and at night it is lit by candles.
Staying at the hotel	Meals and drinks are served on the beach. It's a place to relax and lie by the pool, watching the flamingos which visit the lagoon. But if you like, you can also go horse riding or mountain biking.

El Hotelito Desconocido

 Listen and read

1 Listen and read. Which hotel would you prefer to stay in?

Vocabulary

2 Find words or phrases for the following in the text:
1 pieces of wood on which a building stands
   s̲t̲i̲l̲t̲s̲....
2 rivers of ice
3 three ways of travelling in the snow
4 two things which are used to give light
5 a beautiful place
6 tropical trees
7 colourful birds

Comprehension

3a Write four things that are unusual about each hotel.

The Ice Hotel	The Hotelito Desconocido
It's made of ice.	It's built on stilts.

3b Compare your list with your partner's.

 Listen

4 Which hotel is best for these people, the Ice Hotel (I) or the Hotelito Desconocido (D)?

1 D   2 ☐   3 ☐   4 ☐   5 ☐   6 ☐

Speak

5 Work with a partner. Partner A: You are the receptionist at the Ice Hotel. Answer Partner B's questions. Partner B: You are the receptionist at the Hotelito Desconocido. Answer Partner A's questions.

> A Hello. Can I help you?

> B Yes, I'd like some information about the hotel, please. Where is the hotel exactly?

> B What's the scenery like?

> B What's special about the hotel and what are the rooms like?

> B What activities are available?

Write

6 Imagine you are staying at one of the hotels. Write a postcard to a friend back home.

Hi Ben,
I'm staying at the Ice Hotel in Lapland. It's amazing because
Yesterday we went on snowmobiles. And this morning I've

Let's check

Vocabulary check

1 **Complete the sentences with the correct words.**

blinds	kettle	oven	~~sink~~	toaster	freezer
washing machine	cushion	radiator	sofa	tap	

Can you put the dirty plates in the .**sink**.., please?

1 There's hot chicken and chips in the ....

2 Put some water in the .... and make me a cup of tea.

3 Help yourself to ice cream. It's in the ....

4 Please put all the dirty clothes in the .... and turn it on.

5 Are you having cereal for breakfast or would you like me to put some bread in the .... for you?

6 Have a .... if you're sitting on the floor.

7 Can you turn the heating up? This .... isn't very hot.

8 "Which is the hot ....?" "It's red. The cold one is blue."

9 Can I open the ....? It's very dark in this room.

10 Come and sit on the .... There's room for four people here.

Write your score: .../10

Grammar check

2 **Correct the mistake in each sentence.**
/\ = there's a word missing; X = change one word; ↪ = change the order of two words; * = you must delete one word.

The windows are cleaned once a month Fred Murphy. /\
The windows are cleaned once a month by Fred Murphy.

1 Who was that girl which talked to you after the play? **X**

....

2 I don't like films which they make me cry. *

....

3 Our dog not is allowed on the sofa. ↪

....

4 I know a boy who sister is a famous TV presenter. **X**

....

5 Let's go to that beach you can hire canoes. /\

....

Write your score: .../5

3 **Circle the correct words for each sentence.**

Do you know the boy .**who** runs down this street ev.. day?

A where   B which   **C who**

1 The animals ... at four o'clock.

A fed   B feeding   C are fed

2 I really like the bracelet ... you bought me in India.

A where   B which   C when

3 We ... allowed to use our mobile phones at school.

A not   B aren't   C don't

4 Can you give me back the jeans ... I lent you last week?

A that   B where   C when

5 How much homework ... given at weekends?

A you're   B do you   C are you

6 Let's go to a café ... we can sit outside in the sun.

A which   B that   C where

7 ... always told to tidy the classroom at the end of the day.

A We're   B We   C They

8 Where are the glasses ...?

A keep   B kept   C keeping

9 Have you looked at the magazine ... gave you last week?

A I   B when I   C what I

10 Do you remember the girl ... we met in the park?

A what   B which   C who

Write your score: .../

4 **Make sentences by putting the words in order.**

books / I / laugh / love / make / me / that
I love books that make me laugh.

1 can / go / Let's / mini-golf / park / play / the / to / where / you

....

2 allowed / aren't / at / jewellery / our / school / to / We / wear

....

3 a friend / father / have / is / a film / We / whose / st

....

4 a single / book / for / I'd / one / like / night / to / room

....

5 cleaned / How / is / often / pool / swimming / the /

....

Write your score: ...

Write your total score: .../

8

Illness and injury

1 Listen and complete. 🎧

knee   tooth   back   arm
head   wrist   legs   stomach

Have you hurt yourself?

I've hurt my ....knee.........................

I've cut myself.

I've twisted my ankle.
I've sprained my (1) ....
I've pulled a muscle.
I've broken my (2) ....

I've got a (3) .... ache.
I've got a sore throat.
I've got a temperature.
I've got a cough.
I've got a cold.
I've got a pain in my (4) ....

I've got (5) .... ache.
I've got (6) .... ache.

My (7) .... ache.

I feel ill.   You look pale.
I feel sick.   You're limping.
I feel dizzy.   Your knee's bleeding.

2 Mime an illness or injury. Your partner has to guess what it is.

B You've got a pain in your stomach.

1 I've got a headache.

2 I've got a sore throat.

3 I've got a temperature.

4 I've got a cough.

5 I've got a cold.

6 I've got a pain in my stomach.

7 I've got toothache.

8 I've got backache.

9 I've got flu.

10 I've hurt my knee.

11 I've cut myself.

12 I've sprained my wrist.

13 I've broken my leg.

14 My legs ache.

15 I feel ill.

16 I feel sick.

17 I feel dizzy.

18 You look pale.

19 You're limping.

20 Your knee's bleeding.

Somebody's always late

- Pronouns and adverbs beginning *some-, any-, every-, no-*
- Reported commands
- *If* clauses (2)
- Talking about imaginary situations

  Listen and read

① **Listen and read.**

Becky	When we arrange to do something, somebody's always late. Where is Eddie?
Rachel	Here he is. At last!
Adam	Have you seen Eloisa anywhere, Eddie?
Eddie	No, I haven't.
Rachel	Call her. See if she's still at home.
Becky	There's nobody there.
Rachel	She knows we're meeting at Silver Street Bridge, doesn't she?
Dominic	Does she know Silver Street Bridge?
Adam	If she doesn't know, she'll ask somebody. Everyone knows Silver Street Bridge.
Becky	Look! Isn't that her?
Rachel	She's limping. Something's happened!

Comprehension

② **Choose the correct option: Right (✓) Wrong (✗) It doesn't say (?)**

1 Becky, Rachel, Adam and Dominic are waiting for Eddie and Eloisa. [✓]

2 Eddie is late. [ ]

3 Eloisa arrives before Eddie. [ ]

4 They're all going for a picnic. [ ]

5 Becky phones Eloisa's house. [ ]

6 Eloisa's mum answers the phone. [ ]

7 Eloisa has hurt her knee. [ ]

Grammar focus

Pronouns and adverbs beginning *some-*, *any-*, *every-*, *no-*

some-	any-	every-	no-
somebody/someone	anybody/anyone	everybody/everyone	nobody/no one
something	anything	everything	nothing
somewhere	anywhere	everywhere	nowhere

Generally, use *some-* in affirmative sentences and use *any-* in negative and interrogative sentences:

Something's happened! Have you seen Eloisa anywhere?

How many other words beginning with *some-*, *any-*, *every-* and *no-* can you find in the dialogue?

> There's nobody at home.
> Not: There ~~isn't~~ nobody at home.

Grammar practice

3 **Complete the sentences using words beginning with *some-*, *any-*, *every-* or *no-*.**

1 Are you ready? Have you got ..**everything**... ?

2 I'm hungry, is there .... in the fridge?

3 No, I'm sorry. There's .... in the fridge.

4 .... is here now, so we're ready to go.

5 The bus is full. There's .... to sit.

6 Hello! Is there .... there?

7 We always go to our cousins' for Christmas. Let's go .... different this year.

8 I can't find my mobile phone. I've looked ....

9 I rang the bell but .... answered.

10 Have you seen my keys ....?

11 Urgh! There's .... horrible in my soup.

12 If you go to the information desk, ... will help you.

 Listen

4 **Listen and tick (✓) the correct picture.**

P

B

W
✓

Extra!

5 **Play 'I spy'.**

8

🎧 Listen and read

6 **Listen and read.**

Becky	Eloisa! What happened? What have you done?
Eloisa	I fell off my bike.
Rachel	You've cut your knee. It's bleeding. Does it hurt?
Eloisa	It hurts a bit.
Rachel	You look very pale. Do you feel OK?
Eloisa	I feel a bit dizzy.
Dominic	I'll call my mum. She's a nurse.
Becky	What did your mum say?
Dominic	She told us to take Eloisa to hospital straight away.
Eloisa	Hospital?
Dominic	Yes. She told us not to go on our bikes.
Becky	Well, how are we going to get there?
Dominic	She told us to take a taxi. And she asked me to phone when we arrive.

Comprehension

7 **Answer the questions.**

1 Why was Eloisa late?
 <u>Because she fell off her bike.</u>
2 What has she done?
3 How does she feel?
4 Why does Dominic call his mum?
5 When are they going to take Eloisa to hospital?
6 How are they going to take her to hospital?

Grammar focus

Reported commands
To report a command use *tell/ask* + *(not) to* + infinitive.
'Take Eloisa to hospital.' ⟶ She told us to take Eloisa to hospital.
'Don't go on your bikes.' ⟶ She told us not to go on our bikes.
'Phone when you arrive.' ⟶ She asked me to phone when we arrive.

Remember to use a **name** or an **object pronoun** (me, us, etc.) after *told* and *asked*.
She **asked Dominic** to phone. She **asked him** to phone.

94

Grammar practice

8 **Report these commands. Remember to change the possessive adjectives where necessary.**

1 Mum: 'Tidy your room.'
  Mum asked me to tidy my room.

2 Becky's teacher:'Don't worry about your exam, Becky.'
  Becky's teacher told her
  not to worry about her exam.

3 Rachel: 'Call me later, Becky.'
  Rachel asked Becky ....

4 Becky: 'Don't be late, Eddie.'
  Becky told Eddie ....

5 Eddie: 'Send me a text message, Dominic.'
  Eddie asked Dominic ....

6 Dad: 'Don't spend all your pocket money, Eddie.'
  Eddie's dad told him ....

7 Mum: 'Don't stay out in the sun too long.'
  Mum told me ....

8 Doctor: 'Go to bed and keep warm.'
  The doctor told me ....

 Listen

> Most schools arrange entertainments for the students at the end of term. My school invited a hypnotist to our end-of-term party. It was a great laugh.

9a **Look at the picture. Number the people in the order the hypnotist talks to them.**

Andy ☐   Alice ☐1   Matthew ☐   Patrick ☐
Ben ☐   Emily ☐   Nicola ☐

9b **Listen again. Write the number of the person next to the correct phrase.**

☐ Don't smile.
☐1 Hide under the desk.
☐ Pretend to be a cat.
☐ Pretend to be an aeroplane.
☐ Put your hands up in the air and don't move.
☐ Sing a song from an opera.
☐ Stand on one leg.

9c **Now write sentences about what the hypnotist told people to do.**

He told Alice to hide under the desk.

Speak

10 **Play this game.**

- Tell your partner to do one of the things in Exercise 9b or one of the actions below. Don't let anyone hear.
- Your partner must mime the action.
- The rest of the class has to tell the teacher what you said.

> He told her to touch her toes.

• Play tennis.	• Pretend to be an elephant.
• Brush your teeth.	• Don't laugh.
• Comb your hair.	• Post a letter.
• Wash your hands.	• Pretend to be a ghost.
• Play the guitar in a rock band.	
• Touch your toes.	• Wash the floor.
• Make a cake.	• Pretend to be a firefighter.
• Don't move.	
• Take the dog for a walk.	• Take a photo.

Listen and read

11 **Listen and read.**

Dominic and Rachel have taken Eloisa to the Accident and Emergency department at the hospital. They're in the waiting room.

Dominic	Your mum doesn't know you're here, does she? If I were you, I'd call her. We might be here for ages.
Rachel	By the way, where's your cycle helmet?
Eloisa	I wasn't wearing it. Please don't tell my mum. She'd be very angry if she knew. I'll go and phone her now.
Dominic	If I had my computer game, we could play on it while we're waiting.
Rachel	Well, we can do the quiz in this magazine.
Dominic	OK.
Rachel	Right. 'If you found £50 in the street, what would you do with it? Would you a) take it to the police station? b) spend it? c) leave it where you found it?'
Dominic	I'd take it to the police station. What would you do?
Rachel	I'd spend it immediately! No, I wouldn't. I'd take it to the police station, too.

Comprehension

12 **Write the questions for these answers.**

1 Who is Eloisa with?..................................

   She's with Dominic and Rachel.

2 ....

   They're at the hospital.

3 ....

   She's going to phone her mum.

4 ....

   They're going to do a quiz.

 Listen

13 **What's wrong with Jeremy? What's wrong with Catrina? Listen and tick (✓) the chart.**

		Jeremy	Catrina
1			
2			
3			
4			
5			
6		✓	
7			

Extra!

14 **Now listen to the doctor at the hospital talking to Eloisa. What's wrong with her? What did the doctor tell her to do?**

Grammar focus

If clauses (2)

You can use *if* with the Past simple to talk about what might happen:

if	+ Past simple	+ *would*	+ base form
If	I found £50,	I'd	take it to the police station.

You can also use *if* with the Past simple to talk about things which aren't real or possible:
If I **had** a flying car, I'd fly to school.

Notice that the past tense in the *if* clause does not refer to past time.
You can change the order of the clauses like this:
She'd be very angry if she knew.
If she knew, she'd be very angry.

> With the verb *be*, *were* is often used after *I*, *he* and *she*.

If I were you, I'd call her.
If Mum were here, she wouldn't let us cycle without helmets.

Grammar practice

15a **Match the two halves of the sentences.**

1 If I had a dog, ...f.......
2 If my parents won the lottery,
3 If you had a watch,
4 If my sister went to live in Canada,
5 If I didn't go to bed so late,
6 If people didn't drive so fast,

a) I wouldn't see her for a long time.
b) I'd get up earlier.
c) there wouldn't be so many accidents.
d) they'd buy a house near the sea.
e) you wouldn't always be late.
f) I'd take it for a walk every day.

15b **Complete the sentences by putting the verbs in the correct tenses.**

1 If I .....won........ a lot of money, I ..wouldn't spend.. it all at once. (win, not spend)
2 If I .... a magic carpet, I .... to lots of different countries. (have, fly)
3 If my friend .... me a secret, I .... anybody. (tell, not tell)
4 People .... healthier if they .... (be, not smoke)
5 If the school .... a trip to England, I .... on it. (arrange, go)

Pronunciation

The letters *gh*

16a **Listen. What's the difference in the way *gh* is pronounced in these words?**

1	cough	4	straight
2	enough	5	ghost
3	right		

16b **How do you pronounce these words?**

1	might	4	night
2	through	5	firefighter
3	laugh		

Talk time

17a **Complete the sentences with the correct phrases. Then listen and check.**

a bit	Isn't that ...?	something's happened
at last	~~See if ....~~	straight away

1 .....See if....... dinner's ready.
2 You're here ....
3 .... Penelope Cruz in that car?
4 There's an ambulance outside the house. I think ....
5 I feel .... tired.
6 He looks terrible. Call the doctor ....

17b **Work with a partner. Write six more sentences using the phrases in the box.**

Speak

18 **Work with a partner. Complete the sentences with your own ideas.**

1 If I had a magic carpet, ...
2 If I were a film star, ...
3 If I had one wish, ...
4 If my parents won the lottery, ...

> **A** If I had a magic carpet, I'd fly to the beach every weekend. What about you?

Portfolio

19 Write 50 words beginning: 'If I were a millionaire ...' Go to page 131.

Skills development

Talk Back

Tell us what you think.
Write to us with your opinions.
We're listening!

1 When I was younger, I loved playing with my Barbie doll. I used to think that I would like to look like Barbie when I was older. I now think Barbie is a bad role model for girls because they think they should be like Barbie: tall and blonde, stick-thin legs and a tiny waist. If I had a daughter, I wouldn't give her a Barbie doll for her birthday!

Charlotte Gates, London

2 I think homework is a disgrace. Schools are for schoolwork and home is for fun. If I were a headteacher, I'd ban all homework immediately.

Clark Chapman, Peterborough

3 My sister and I are very angry about racism in football. If we didn't have players from other countries playing in England, our clubs would not be so successful. In our view, everyone is equal. If we didn't have racism in football, many more people would enjoy it.

Sophie Holt, via e-mail

4 I've lived in London for several years, and I've only ever seen a few stars at night, because the street lights are so bright. I think it's called 'light pollution'. I used to live in Cornwall. There, the sky was full of stars every night. Wouldn't it be better if we didn't have so many street lights in big cities?

Zoe Lee, London

 Listen and read

1 Listen and read. Each person sent in a picture with their letter. But who sent which picture?

1 Sophie ....

3 ....

2 ....

4 ....

5

How can people be so cruel to animals? I was looking through a book and I found a page about tigers. There are only about 150 Siberian tigers in the whole world. Why? Because they are killed for their fur and their bones are used in some types of medicine. If people didn't buy these things, tigers wouldn't be killed.

Josh Ratcliffe, Hampshire

6

Three times this week, cars have nearly knocked me off my bike. If people got out of their cars and onto their bikes, the roads would be a lot safer, and the air would be cleaner. Road safety and air pollution affect everybody.

Anika Rahman, Manchester

5...............................

6...............................

Vocabulary

2 Try to guess the meaning of these words and phrases from the context.

1	role model	5	ban
2	stick-thin	6	successful
3	a tiny waist	7	street lights
4	a disgrace	8	knocked me off my bike

Comprehension

3 Say what each person is writing about. Use words or phrases from the text.

Charlotte's writing about Barbie dolls as role models.

Listen

4 You're going to hear six people talking about the same topics as the letters in Exercise 1.

Read Charlotte's letter again. Then listen to Louise. Does she agree with Charlotte?

Do the same for the other people: read each letter again then listen.

		Agrees	Disagrees
1	Louise		✓
2	Rachel		
3	Sanjay		
4	Adam		
5	James		
6	Elliot		

Speak

5 Work with a partner. On each issue, say who you agree with and give your reasons.

> A I agree with Charlotte about Barbie dolls. I think that ... because ...

Write

6 Now write a letter to *Talk Back*. Give your views on one of the issues.

Dear Talk Back,

I think Barbie dolls are really stupid. They're expensive and they aren't good role models for girls.

Culture spot
Ireland, Scotland and Wales

 Listen and read

1 Listen and read.

Scotland, Wales and Northern Ireland, together with England, make up the United Kingdom, but they are separate countries with their own cultures and traditions.

Ireland

Ireland is made up of Northern Ireland and the Republic of Ireland. It is sometimes called the 'Emerald Isle' because the countryside is so green and beautiful. There are strong traditions of music, poetry and story-telling in Ireland. Irish bands, such as U2 and Westlife, are known everywhere. Fiddles (violins), pipes and banjos are all used in traditional Irish folk music. A lot of this music isn't written down. It's passed from one musician to another.

In the 1800s most Irish people lived on small farms and ate mainly potatoes. But when the potato crop failed in the 1840s more than 750,000 people died of hunger and thousands of people emigrated from Ireland to the USA and other countries.

St Patrick's Day (March 17th) is celebrated by Irish people all over the world.

Scotland

The Scots have invented many of the things we use every day, like the telephone and the TV. They have traditions which are different from English traditions. For instance, on New Year's Eve (December 31st) everyone gets dressed up and there are parties everywhere. It's called Hogmanay. Bagpipes are often played and traditional clothes, such as kilts, are worn. Kilts are made of wool in a special design called tartan and they are worn by men. Each tartan belongs to a different 'clan' or family group.

Wales

Wales also has strong traditions. There is an international festival, called *the Eisteddfod*, which is held every year. There are competitions in singing, poetry and music. The Welsh language is taught in schools in Wales and Welsh is spoken at home in some areas. The Welsh language sounds and looks very different from English. Rugby is the national sport.

Vocabulary

2 **Find the following in the text.**

Ireland

1 a popular name for Ireland   The 'Emerald Isle'

2 three traditional Irish musical instruments   ....

Scotland

3 the Scottish word for a family group   ....

4 a traditional pattern   ....

Wales

5 the language spoken in Wales   ....

6 the name of the international festival of music and poetry   ....

Speak

3 **Work with a partner. Ask and answer these questions.**

Partner A

1 What's New Year's Eve called in Scotland?

2 What are kilts made of?

3 Who are they worn by?

4 What musical instrument is played on special occasions in Scotland?

5 What do people do at *the Eisteddfod*?

Partner B

1 Which sport is very popular in Wales?

2 If you went to school in Wales, which languages would you learn?

3 Why is Ireland called the 'Emerald Isle'?

4 Why did people emigrate from Ireland in the 1840s?

5 If you were Irish, which day would you celebrate?

Write

4 **Write about your country's traditions. Start by making notes under these headings:**

- famous writers, musicians and artists
- other famous people, e.g. inventors
- special events or occasions
- other traditions
- special clothes
- food
- language: regional words and expressions

Sut mae, Gareth Evans w fy enw i. Yr ywf i'n dod Gaerdydd. Rwyn siarad Cymraeg a Saesneg a rwyn hoffi rygbi!

=

Hello! My name's Gareth Evans. I'm from Cardiff. I speak Welsh and English. And I love rugby.

Let's check

Vocabulary check

1 **Complete the sentences with the correct words.**

bleeding	flu	throat
dizzy	headache	twisted

Anna's got a sore ...throat... ....

1 Ella feels ....

2 Sue has .... her ankle.

3 Jade's knee is ....

4 Rita has got a ....

5 Nina has got ....

Write your score: ..../5

Grammar check

2 **Make sentences by putting the words in order.**

I / go / hair / not / out / to / told / wet / with / you
I told you not to go out with wet hair.

1 but / can't / everywhere / find / glasses / I still / I've / looked / my

....
....

2 dive off / gave you / If I / you / the top board / £20 / would / ?

....
....

3 anybody / are / Do / know / parents / really / strict / whose / you / ?

....
....

4 ask / Do / help / housework / your parents / the / to / you / with / ?

....
....

5 fly, / could / If / you / you / fly to first / where / would / ?

....
....

Write your score: ..../5

3 **Choose the correct words for each sentence.**

"I think you know ..**everybody**.., don't you?"
"Yes, we're all in the same class."

A anybody   **B** nobody   **C** everybody

1 If you had a horse, where … you keep it?
A will   **B** would   **C** do

2 I don't know … who lives in Grange Road.
A nobody   **B** somebody   **C** anybody

3 Why … everybody looking at the sky?
A is   **B** are   **C** does

4 The doctor … stay in bed for two days.
A told   **B** told to   **C** told me to

5 You aren't ill. There's … wrong with you.
A everything   **B** nothing   **C** anything

6 My mother asked me … the rubbish out.
A taking   **B** took   **C** to take

7 If you … Jennifer Lopez, what would you say to her?
A will meet   **B** meet   **C** met

8 There's a bookshop … in this street, but I'm not sure where.
A everywhere   **B** anywhere   **C** somewhere

9 The dentist told her … any sweets.
A to eat not   **B** not to eat   **C** to not eating

10 My cat is like a dog. She follows me … .
A nowhere   **B** somewhere   **C** everywhere

Write your score: ..../1(

Correct the mistake in each sentence.

4 /\ = there's a word missing; X = change one word; ↪ = change the order of two words; * = you must delete one word.

If you can meet anyone in the world, who would you choose? **X**

if you could meet anyone in the world, who would you choose?

1 What you would do if you won £1,000? ↪

....

2 My father told to me not to call him at work. *

....

3 What would you do if you will found a snake in your bed? *

....

4 Mum asked me turn the washing machine on. /\

....

5 I don't know nobody who likes long bus trips. **X**

....

Write your score:
Write your total score: .

How good are you?

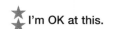  ★ I'm not very good at this.   ★★ I'm OK at this.   ★★★ I'm good at this.

Tick (✓) the correct boxes.

		★	★★	★★★
READING I can understand:				
a conversation about people moving to Britain	*She's coming to do some research at the university.*			
a conversation about a house to rent	*This is the kitchen. It's got a cooker, a fridge and …*			
a letter booking rooms at a hotel	*I would like to book two rooms for two weeks …*			
hotel brochures	*The Ice Hotel is the most unusual hotel you'll ever stay in.*			
a conversation after a minor accident	*You look very pale. Do you feel OK?*			
letters to a teen magazine	*How can people be so cruel to animals?*			
an article about the United Kingdom	*The Welsh language is taught in schools in Wales and Welsh is spoken at home in some areas.*			
LISTENING I can understand:				
people phoning to book hotel rooms	*Is breakfast included?*			
people talking about their ideal hotel or holiday	*My favourite holiday? Lying on the beach with a nice cool drink by my side!*			
people playing 'I Spy'	*I spy with my little eye, something beginning with …*			
a hypnotist giving orders	*Patrick, pretend to be a cat.*			
people agreeing or disagreeing with letters to a teen magazine	*I'm calling about Kirsty's letter. I've read about tigers too. And it's terrible.*			
WRITING I can write:				
a letter to a hotel asking about accommodation	*I would like to book two rooms for two nights …*			
a postcard describing an unusual hotel	*I'm staying at the Ice Hotel in Lapland. It's amazing because …*			
about what I'd do if I were a millionaire	*If I were a millionaire, I'd buy a cinema and show my favourite films in it.*			
a letter giving my views on an issue	*I think people should stop being cruel to animals.*			
about traditions in my own region	*On August 15th it is traditional in my town to …*			
SPEAKING I can:				
identify people and things in photos	*This is the shoe which Cinderella lost at the ball.*			
role-play a receptionist and a guest making a phone booking	*I'd like to book two rooms for two nights, please.*			
role-play a receptionist and someone asking for information about a hotel	*What's special about the hotel and what are the rooms like?*			
play 'I spy'	*I spy with my little eye something beginning with P.*			
guess from a mime what somebody was told to do	*He told her to touch her toes.*			
talk about what I would do in a given situation	*If I had a magic carpet, I'd get on it and fly to Brazil.*			
agree and disagree with letters to a teen magazine	*I agree with Anika. It's true that doctors need to use cars. But most other people could use a bike in town.*			

Vocabulary groups

Write three more words in each vocabulary group.

Things in the kitchen	fridge	cooker	....	....	....
Things in the living area	chairs	table	....	....	....
Illness nouns	cough	cold	....	....	....
Illness verbs	I've hurt	I feel	....	....	....

Module 5

Grammar

Past perfect simple
Reported statements
Say and *tell*
If clauses (3)
Present perfect continuous
Past passive simple
Reported questions

Vocabulary

Town and country
Eating out

Communication

Arranging to meet
Ordering a meal in a restaurant

Pronunciation

Weak forms of verbs
Weak forms of prepositions

Culture spot

The most popular food on
the planet

Town and country

9

1 Listen to Robert and number the places in the order he mentions them. You can listen more than once.

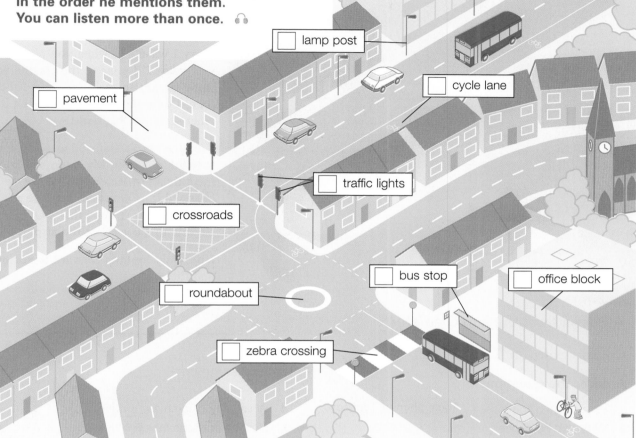

- [ ] T-junction
- [1] tower block
- [ ] lamp post
- [ ] cycle lane
- [ ] pavement
- [ ] traffic lights
- [ ] crossroads
- [ ] roundabout
- [ ] bus stop
- [ ] office block
- [ ] zebra crossing

2 Now listen to Vanessa and number the places in the order she mentions them. You can listen more than once.

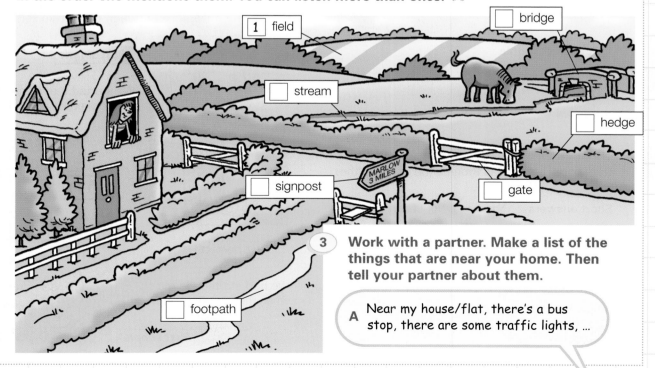

- [1] field
- [ ] bridge
- [ ] stream
- [ ] hedge
- [ ] signpost
- [ ] gate
- [ ] footpath

MARLOW
3 MILES

3 Work with a partner. Make a list of the things that are near your home. Then tell your partner about them.

A Near my house/flat, there's a bus stop, there are some traffic lights, …

I'd gone to the cinema

- Past perfect simple
- Arranging to meet
- Reported statements
- *Say* and *tell*
- *If* clauses (3)

🎧 Listen and read

1 Listen and read.

A Scene from the film *Gladiator*

Hi Adam

Sorry I wasn't in when you phoned yesterday. I'd gone to the cinema with some friends to see *Gladiator*. I'd already seen it on video but I hadn't seen it at the cinema. It was brilliant!

I'm arriving at Stansted airport on Friday July 9th at 11.30. My mum had booked me a ticket to Heathrow but we've changed it to Stansted, because it's closer to Cambridge. I hope that's OK. Will you be able to meet me at the airport?

I'm really looking forward to seeing you and the others.

Tommaso

Comprehension

2 Answer the questions.

1 Who phoned Tommaso? ..Adam phoned Tommaso....
2 When did he phone?
3 What did Tommaso think of *Gladiator*?

4 Which day is Tommaso arriving?
5 How is Tommaso travelling?
6 Where is Stansted?

Grammar focus

Past perfect simple

Affirmative	I You He/She/It	had (gone).
Negative	We You They	hadn't (gone).
Questions	Had I/you/he/she/it/we/you/they (gone)?	
Short answers	Yes, I had./No, I hadn't.	

Use the Past perfect when you want to make it clear that one thing happened before another in the past.

Look at this sentence:
Tommaso had gone to the cinema when Adam phoned.

Which happened first?

☐ Adam phoned.

☐ Tommaso went to the cinema.

What's the difference between these two sentences?

Past simple

We **started** the match when the goalkeeper **arrived**.

Past simple

Past perfect

We **had started** the match when the goalkeeper **arrived**.

Past simple

Grammar practice

3a **Complete the sentences with the verbs in brackets in the correct tenses: Past simple and Past perfect simple.**

1 David ..**wanted**.... (want) to go out for a pizza but ..**I'd invited**. (invite) friends for a meal.

2 Mum .... (need) the car but Dad .... (take) it to the garage.

3 Ben .... (not finish) his work when Danny .... (arrive) to play football.

4 We .... (give) him a computer game for his birthday but his parents .... (buy) it for him the week before.

5 They .... (not want) to go to Sicily because they .... (go) there before.

3b **Combine the sentences as in the example. Start your answers with the second sentence.**

1 You left at 6 o'clock. I called to say goodbye.
..**I called to say goodbye**.. but **you had left**..........
.**at 6 o'clock**.........

2 The bus left early. I got to the bus stop on time.
.... but ....

3 We had a big breakfast. We weren't hungry.
.... because ....

4 I saw the film on Thursday. I didn't want to go with them to the cinema.
.... because ....

5 He went to bed. He didn't answer the phone.
.... because ....

6 The concert didn't start on time. We arrived late.
.... but luckily ....

3c **Combine each pair of sentences using the Past perfect simple and *when*, as in the example.**

1 I ate all the chocolates. Then you arrived.
.**I had eaten all the chocolates when you arrived.**

2 I went to bed. Then you phoned.
....

3 We left. Then our cousins arrived.
....

4 He stole five cars. Then the police caught him.
....

5 Dad did all the washing up. Then I offered to help him.
....

Read and speak

4 **Try this quiz with your partner.**
Partner A: Give Partner B these clues. See if he/she can guess what you are describing.

1 You wait here for the bus.

B   A bus stop

2 Cars go round it.
3 They're red, orange and green.
4 You walk on it in the town.
5 You can chain your bike to it.
6 It's black and white. You cross the road here.

Partner B. Give Partner A these clues. See if he/she can guess what you are describing.

1 It's a place where you keep cows and horses.

A   A field

2 It's green and you find it round Number 1.
3 It's a tall building where people live.
4 It's a small river.
5 It's a building where lots of people work.
6 You must close it when you go out of a field.

Extra!

5 **Read Adam's e-mail. Write a similar description of where your house is.**

```
untitled
Send Now  Send Later        Signature ▼  Options ▼

Hi Tommaso
Guess what? I've found a street
plan on the web which shows my
house! It's in Summerfield Road,
near the roundabout on Newnham
Road. It's quite near the park.
There's a footpath across the
park which goes to the river.
Have a look. Can you see it?

Adam
```

9

🎧 Listen and read

6 **Listen and read.**

Eddie	I phoned Adam. He said he'd had an e-mail from Tommaso.
Rachel	He's coming soon, isn't he?
Eddie	Yes. He said he'd be in Cambridge on July 9th.
Becky	Oh, great! We can show him around.
Eddie	He told Adam he wanted to go punting.
Rachel	Punting?
Eddie	And he said that he was looking forward to seeing us all. Especially you and Becky.
Becky	Did he?
Eddie	No.
Becky	I hate you, Eddie!

Comprehension

7 **Answer the questions.**

1 Who phoned Adam?
   <u>Eddie phoned Adam.</u>

2 Who sent an e-mail to Adam?

3 When will Tommaso arrive in Cambridge?

4 What's Becky's plan?

5 What activity does Tommaso want to do?

6 Why do you think Eddie teases Becky about Tommaso?

You can omit *that* in reported sentences.

He told Adam (that) he wanted to go punting.
And he said (that) he was looking forward to seeing us all.

Grammar focus

Reported statements

When you report what someone said, you usually change the tense:

am/are/is	→	was/were
have/has	→	had
will/would	→	would
can/could	→	could
do/does	→	did
Present simple	→	Past simple
Past simple/Present perfect	→	Past perfect

Tommaso: 'I **want** to go punting.'
He told Adam he **wanted** to go punting.

Tommaso: 'I**'m** looking forward to seeing you all.'
He said that he **was** looking forward to seeing them all.

Tommaso: 'I**'ll** be in Cambridge on July 9th.'
He said he**'d be** in Cambridge on July 9th.

Adam: 'I **had**/I**'ve had** an e-mail from Tommaso.'
He said he**'d had** an e-mail from Tommaso.

You must use a name or an object pronoun after *tell*:
He **told Adam** he wanted to go punting./He **told him** he wanted to go punting.

You don't use a name or an object pronoun after *say*:
He **said** he wanted to go punting.

Grammar practice

8 **Write a caption for each picture.**

1 She said she hadn't seen his chocolates.

2 He ....

3 They ....

4 He ....

5 He ....

6 She ....

9a **Complete the reported statements.**

1 You're always late.
She said that he was always late.

2 I don't want to go shopping.
He told her that he ....

3 We've walked all the way from Eddie's house.
He said that they ....

4 I've already done it.
She said that she ....

5 I'll give you some extra pocket money.
She told him that she ....

6 I love being with animals.
He said that he ....

7 She's coming to Cambridge with her parents.
He told them that she ....

8 I feel a bit dizzy.
She told her that she ....

Extra!

9b **Look at the statements again. Can you remember who was talking, and who they were talking to and one more detail?**

1 Becky was talking to Eddie. They were having breakfast.

Speak

10 **Play 'Chinese Whispers'.**

9

Read and listen

11a **Look at the photos and put the dialogue in the correct order.**

Becky	If you hadn't been so silly, you wouldn't have fallen in!
Dominic	It's OK. I've got a spare T-shirt in my rucksack.
Eddie	Thanks, Dom!

Adam	Where did you leave your bikes?
Rachel	We chained them to a lamp post by the bridge.
Tommaso	How do we get down to the river?
Becky	Oh, you just go through the gate and walk along the footpath.

Eloisa	Look, the signpost says: 'Grantchester 3 miles'.
Rachel	I don't think we've got time to go to Grantchester.
Adam	If we'd started earlier, we'd have been there by now
Tommaso	It doesn't matter, it's beautiful here.
Eddie	It's very romantic, isn't it, Becky?
Becky	Stop it, Eddie. I'll push you in if you don't shut up.
Adam	Mind that branch, Eddie!

11b **Listen and check.**

Comprehension

12 **Answer the questions.**

1 What have the girls done with their bikes?
   They've chained them to a lamp post.
2 How do you get to the river from the bridge?
3 Why can't they go to Grantchester?
4 Does Becky push Eddie into the water?
5 What does Eddie hit?
6 What happens to Eddie?
7 How does Dominic help Eddie?

Grammar focus

If clauses (3)

We can use *if* clauses to talk about things that might have happened but didn't happen:

| *If* + Past perfect | *would have* *could have* | + past participle |

If we'd started earlier, we**'d have been** there by now.
(But we didn't start earlier, so we're not there.)

If you hadn't been so silly, you **wouldn't have fallen** in!
(But you were silly, so you fell in.)

If **we'd** started earlier, **we'd** have been there by now.
↓ ↓
we had   we would

110

13a Complete the sentence with *would have* or *could have* + the past participle of the verb in brackets.

1 If it had been sunny last week, we
   <u>would have gone</u> sailing. (would/go)

2 If I'd had enough money, I .... the new Shakira CD. (could/buy)

3 If it hadn't rained, we .... to the beach. (would/go)

4 If Tommaso had been in Cambridge last week, they .... him to the match. (could/take)

5 If he hadn't run all the way, he .... at school on time. (would/not arrive)

6 If I'd worn a jacket, I .... so cold. (would/not be)

13b Complete the sentences.

1 If he hadn't been so silly, he <u>wouldn't have fallen</u> off his bike.

2 If he <u>hadn't fallen</u> off his bike, he wouldn't have gone to hospital.

3 If he hadn't gone to hospital, he .... the doctor.

4 If he hadn't met the doctor, he .... in love.
   If he hadn't fallen in love, he wouldn't have married the doctor.

5 If he .... the doctor, he wouldn't have had a son.

6 If he hadn't had a son, he .... so silly.

7 If he hadn't been so silly, he .... off his bike.

Pronunciation
Weak forms of verbs

14 Listen to each word. Then listen to the same word in a sentence. Practise the sentences with a partner.

1 was   He **was** looking forward to seeing us all.
2 were Did Adam tell you we **were** going punting?
3 can   We **can** show you around.
4 could Eddie asked Dominic if he **could** borrow his T-shirt.
5 have If you hadn't been so silly you wouldn't **have** fallen in.
6 had   If it **had** been sunny we would have gone sailing.
7 do   **Do** you want to go punting?
8 does How long **does** it take to get to Grantchester?

Talk time

15 Use the phrases in the box to complete the letter. Then listen and check.

I hope that's OK.   I can't wait!
Looking forward to seeing you   especially ...
We can show you around.

Dear Alexandra,

My mum and I will be at Waterloo Station at 11 o'clock on Wednesday. <u>I hope that's OK.</u> We're going to spend the day in London. .... There are some great places to see and there are some lovely shops, ... in Covent Garden. And we've got tickets to go on the London Eye. ....

.... again.

Love from

Briony

Speak

16 Work with a partner. Role-play a phone conversation with a friend who is coming to your country. Arrange where and when to meet. Say what you're going to do. Try to use each of the phrases in Exercise 15.

A OK, so where will I meet you and at what time?

B Well, I'll be at (the airport) at (2.15) on (Friday). I hope that's OK.

Big city to beach

Last year 14-year-old Zoe Larrad moved from Manchester to Christchurch in Dorset – from the big city to the beach. She has been in Christchurch for six months now and we went to meet her.

 Listen and read

1 **Listen and read.**

Zoe's story

"I'd lived in Manchester since I was born and I didn't want to leave. But my mum, who's a bank manager, got a new job in Dorset and we had to go. My dad's a lorry driver so he doesn't mind where we live. Anyway, he'd always wanted to live by the sea.

On the day we moved, I cried and cried. I didn't want to leave my school friends, especially my best friend Emma. I had known her all my life.

We moved on July 31st and I didn't see anyone my own age for a month. I didn't know where to go to meet people. Then one day there was a group of girls across the street.

My dad said he was going to go over and invite them in. I went out straight away! If I hadn't gone and talked to them, my dad would have gone out and said something like: 'Come and meet my daughter. She doesn't know anyone here.' That would have been really embarrassing.

I got talking to them and I asked, 'Where do you hang out?' They said, 'Here. This is it.' Back in Manchester we used to get dressed up and go bowling or to an under-18s club night. Here we meet at the beach or in the fields near my house. It's not as exciting but it's safer here, so I can stay out later.

My first day at my new school was hell. I had to stand in front of 29 people and say my name about five times because they couldn't understand my accent. Luckily, I met Katie who was also new, so we could learn about the place together.

I still miss my old mates. But I think my new friendships will be just as strong as my old ones.

Would I go back to Manchester if I had the chance? That's a difficult question. If you'd asked me when I first arrived, I would have said 'Yes' straight away. But I think I'd miss my life here now."

Comprehension

2 Answer the questions.

1 How long had Zoe lived in Manchester? .14 years....
2 Why did she move to Christchurch?
3 How long had Zoe and Emma been friends?
4 Why was Zoe unhappy when she first arrived?
5 What's different about life in Dorset and life in Manchester for young people?

6 What was the problem on Zoe's first day at her new school?
7 Why was she happy to meet Katie?
8 How do you think Zoe feels now about her life in Dorset?

Listen

3a Who's talking?

• Zoe
• Katie
• Emma
• Zoe's mother
• Zoe's father

1 .Katie....

3b Listen again. Which does each person prefer, the city or the beach?

1 .Katie - city....

Speak

4 Have you ever moved from one town or region to another?

Yes

**Tell the class about your experience.
Use these questions to help you prepare:**

Where did you use to live?

How long had you lived there before you moved?

What was it like?

What did you like about it?

What didn't you like about it?

No

What are the advantages of living in a city? What are the advantages of living in the country/near the beach? Prepare a few sentences to give your views. Use these notes to help you:

I prefer living in the city/in the country/near the beach.
   It's ...

more exciting	There is ...
boring	nothing to do,
safer	more traffic
quieter	There are ...
friendly	fields and beaches,
easier to meet your friends	cinemas, under - 18s clubs

Write

5 Write a paragraph about your experience.

I.used.to.live.in.Faro..I.lived.there.for.seven.......
years before I moved to Lisbon. ....

Write a paragraph giving your views.

I.prefer living.in.the.country..It's.safer.than.
the.city,.and.the.people.are.friendlier..............

Let's check

Vocabulary check

1 **Match the words to the sentences.**

bridge	hedge	lamp post
pavement	~~signpost~~	stream

It tells you the way to go. .signpost..

1 It allows you to cross a river. ....

2 It gives light to a street at night. ....

3 It's a very small river. ....

4 It's next to the road and people walk on it.
....

5 There's sometimes one around a garden.
....

Write your score: .../5

2 **Match the words to the pictures.**

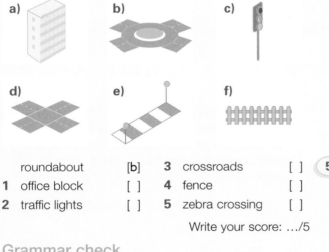

roundabout	[b]	**3** crossroads	[ ]
1 office block	[ ]	**4** fence	[ ]
2 traffic lights	[ ]	**5** zebra crossing	[ ]

Write your score: .../5

Grammar check

3 **Correct the mistake in each sentence.**
/\ = there's a word missing; X = change one
word; ↪ = change the order of two words;
***** = you must delete one word.**

I said her that we would be late. **X**
.I told her that we would be late..........................

1 When I got to the party, Maria already left. **/**
....

2 She said that had she left her phone at home. **↪**
....

3 If you'd of seen her face, you would have laughed. *****
....

4 I said I will be there at seven but I was an hour late. **X**
....

5 You wouldn't met me if you'd gone to a different school. **/**
....

Write your score: .../5

4 **Choose the correct words for each sentence.**

When I got there they ..had already.. started playing.
  A already   **B** were already **C** had already

1 If I … my camera with me, I'd have taken a photo.
  A had   **B** had had   **C** was having

2 She … me that they would be late.
  A told   **B** said   **C** is telling

3 I didn't pay because I … my purse at home.
  A had left   **B** was leaving **C** leave

4 If you had put on more sunscreen, you … burnt.
  A didn't get **B** wouldn't have got **C** wouldn't ge

5 She said she … tell me because it was a secret.
  A wouldn't **B** can't   **C** doesn't

6 He went home early because he …left something in th
oven.
  A was   **B** had   **C** is

7 You said you … going to make a cake.
  A are   **B** were   **C** was

8 It would have been fun if I hadn't … myself.
  A of hurt **B** have hurt **C** hurt

9 My parents … they would be back quite late.
  A told   **B** said   **C** say

10 We'd have bought a present if we … .
  A knew   **B** would know **C** had known

Write your score: .../1

5 **Make sentences by putting the words in**
order. Add commas where necessary.

a / funny / it / film / said / They / very / was
.They said it was a very funny film..............

1 day / every / he / He / me / told / would / write
....
....

2 a lot / back to / but / changed / had / He went / it / his
village
....
....

3 colour / couldn't / eyes / his / of / remember / said /
she / She / the
....
....

4 called / had / have / He / he'd / if / number / would /
your
....
....

5 at home / because / didn't / get / had / He / he / his
phone / left / my text message
....
....

Write your score: .../5

Write your total score: .../30

10

Eating out

1 Listen and follow. 🎧

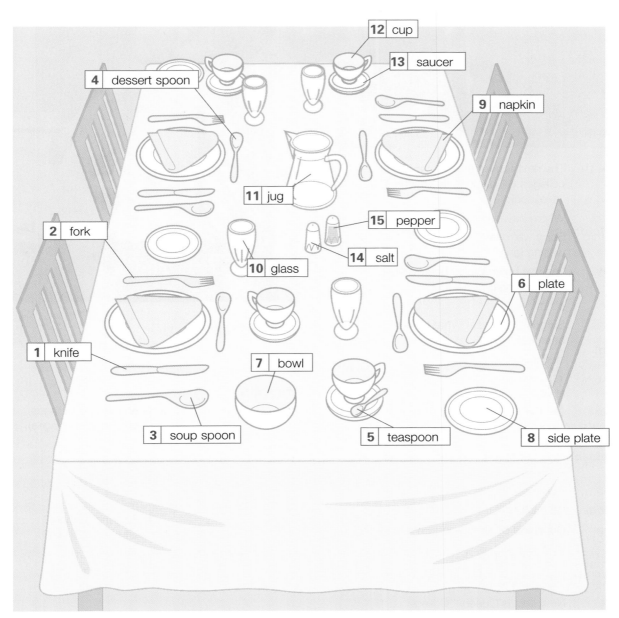

2 Work with a partner. Cover the picture. How many items on the table can you remember?

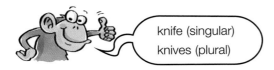

knife (singular)
knives (plural)

3 Listen. Put a tick (✓) next to the positive comments and a cross (✗) next to the negative comments. 🎧

1	delicious ✓	7	overdone
2	tasty	8	fresh
3	too salty	9	too spicy
4	nice	10	sweet
5	just right	11	superb
6	burnt		

10

We've been waiting here for ages

- Present perfect continuous
- Past passive simple
- Reported questions
- Ordering a meal in a restaurant

🎧 Listen and read

1 **Listen and read.**

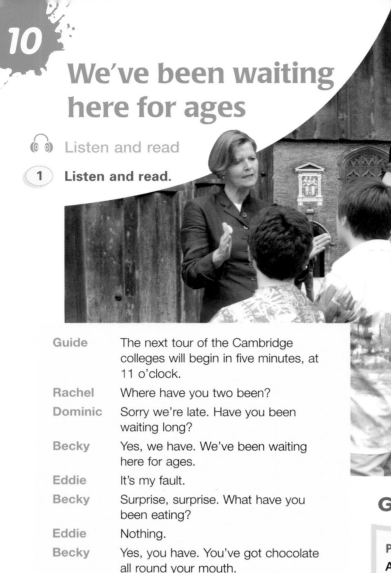

Guide	The next tour of the Cambridge colleges will begin in five minutes, at 11 o'clock.
Rachel	Where have you two been?
Dominic	Sorry we're late. Have you been waiting long?
Becky	Yes, we have. We've been waiting here for ages.
Eddie	It's my fault.
Becky	Surprise, surprise. What have you been eating?
Eddie	Nothing.
Becky	Yes, you have. You've got chocolate all round your mouth.
Eddie	Oh. Oh, yes, I stopped for an ice cream on the way here.
Tommaso	How long have you been learning English?
Eloisa	Five years.
Tommaso	So have I.
Eloisa	Dominic's been learning English since he was five.
Tommaso	I hope the tour guide will speak slowly.
Rachel	I'm sure she will.
Guide	Now, this is Queens' College ...

Comprehension

2 **Complete the summary.**

(1) ....Eddie and Dominic........... are late. Eddie had (2) .... on the way into town. The group are going to go on a tour of (3) .... with a guide. The tour starts at (4) .... Rachel is sure the guide will speak (5) .... They're all standing outside (6) .... College.

Grammar focus

Present perfect continuous

Affirmative

I've/You've/We've/They've	been (waiting for ages).
He's/She's/It's	been (waiting for ages).

Negative

I haven't	been (waiting).
He hasn't	been (waiting).

Questions

Have you	been (waiting long)?
Has he	been (waiting long)?

Short answers

Yes, I have.	No, I haven't.
Yes, he has.	No, he hasn't.

Present tense of *have*	+ *been* +	*-ing* form of the verb
We**'ve**	**been**	**waiting** here for ages.

You can use the Present perfect continuous instead of the Present perfect simple when you want to emphasize a period of time:

We**'ve been waiting** here for ages.

You can also use the *Present perfect continuous* when you can see the results of a past action:

What **have** you **been eating**?
(I can see you have been eating something.)

You**'ve been eating** chocolate ice cream.
(You've got chocolate all round your mouth.)

Grammar practice

3 Complete the sentences with the verbs in the box in the correct form of the Present perfect continuous.

have	play	swim	not come
learn	~~run~~	not answer	not listen

1 You look hot! You.'ve been running..

2 Her English is very good. She .... English since she was very young.

3 You say you can't see the blackboard. How long .... you .... problems?

4 Why is your hair wet? .... you ....?

5 Leanne's a bit upset. Tom .... her e-mails.

6 What's the matter with Lisa and Joanna? They .... to dance class recently.

7 I've told you three times that we're going out for a pizza tonight! You .... to me.

8 I'm a bit tired because I.............................. .... in a lot of matches recently.

Write

4 Look at the pictures. What have they been doing?

1 She's been cleaning the kitchen.......

2 ....

Listen

5 Laura's friend Ella phones her for a chat. Listen and answer the questions.

1 What has Laura been doing at school?
  She's been rehearsing for the school play..

2 What has Laura been doing at home? Why?

3 Why can't Ella use her computer?

4 Where has Ella been sleeping?

5 Why does Laura think Ella is lucky?

Extra!

6 Work with a partner. Ask and answer.

1 How long have you been learning English? Do you find it easy or difficult?

2 Have you been living in (*your town*) for a long time? What are the good things about it?

3 What have you been doing at weekends recently? What's your favourite weekend activity?

4 Have you been watching (*name of a TV series*)? *If the answer is 'Yes':* What do you think of it? *If the answer is 'No':* Have you been watching any other TV series?

3 ....

4 ....

5 ....

7 **Listen and read.**

Guide Now, this is Queens' College. The bridge behind you is called the Wooden Bridge. It was built in 1749. The Chapel and the Library were built much earlier, in 1448.

Becky Were girls allowed to study here in those days?

Guide No, they weren't. Girls weren't accepted at Queens' College until 1980.

Rachel 1980! That's disgraceful!

Adam I expect it wasn't much fun even for boys hundreds of years ago.

Guide Well, the gates of the college were locked at 8 p.m. in winter and 9 p.m. in summer. And students weren't allowed to have long hair.

Guide And now we come to King's College, with its famous chapel. King Henry VI decided to build a college here in 1440. But the land was covered with houses and shops, so they were all knocked down to make space. The foundation stone of the chapel was laid on 25 July 1446 by the king himself.

Eddie History's very interesting ... but it makes you hungry!

Dominic Mmm. I'm looking forward to our meal this evening.

Comprehension

8 **Answer the questions.**

1 Which college do the group visit first?
  Queens' College...

2 Which two buildings at Queens' College does the guide mention?

3 Which building at King's College does the guide mention?

4 Which king is King's College named after?

5 When did the building of King's College begin?

6 What are the group going to do this evening?

Grammar focus

Past simple passive

To form the Past simple passive, use the Past simple of *be + the past participle*: *was/were + built*:

The Wooden Bridge **was built** in 1749.
The Chapel and the Library **were built** in 1448.

Look at the dialogue and find:
1 a question in the Past passive.
2 two negative statements in the Past passive.

Like the Present passive, the Past passive is used:

• when we talk about formal arrangements and rules:
  Students **weren't allowed** to have long hair.

• when it's not relevant to specify a particular person:
  The Chapel and the Library **were built** in 1448.

Find another example of each kind of use.

Grammar practice

9a **Complete the sentences with *was/were*.**

1 The plane ....**was**..... delayed for three hours.

2 Rome ....n't built in a day.

3 .... your grandparents taught English at school?

4 No, they ....n't. They .... taught Latin and French.

5 My mother ....n't allowed to wear trousers to school.

6 The winning goal .... scored from a penalty.

9b **Complete the sentences using the verbs in the Past passive.**

1 The heating wasn't working so we ...**were sent**... home from school. (send)

2 The field .... with snow. (cover)

3 Our cat .... 50 miles away! (find)

4 We .... that the match was cancelled. (not tell)

5 Where .... *The Lord of the Rings* ....? (film)

6 *The Stay of King Arthur* ....
into a film last year. (make)

Read and speak

10a **Work with a partner. Take turns to choose a category. Ask and answer the questions.**

Quiz time

Firsts

1 Where were the first Olympic Games held?
a) In France.   b) In Greece.

2 When was the first VW Beetle made?
a) the 1940s.   b) the 1980s.

3 When were the first films shown to a paying audience?
a) In 1895.   b) In 1927.

4 Where were the first handwritten newspapers produced?
a) In Rome.   b) In China.

Plants and animals

1 In Aztec Mexico, cocoa beans were used as
a) money.   b) animal food.

2 Which animals were taken to the Americas by the Spanish?
a) Cats.   b) Horses.

3 Which animal was Cleopatra killed by?
a) A snake.   b) A tiger.

4 Tomatoes and potatoes weren't known in Europe until
a) the 14th century.   b) the 17th century.

Food

1 Coffee was introduced to Europe
a) in 1600.   b) in 950.

2 The sandwich was invented by
a) an American.   b) an Englishman.

3 When were hamburgers first eaten in the USA?
a) In 1900.   b) In 1950.

4 Where was the world's biggest pizza made?
a) In South Africa.   b) In Italy.

The Arts

1 *Romeo and Juliet* was written by
a) Dante.   b) Shakespeare.

2 The Statue of Liberty was designed by
a) Gustave Eiffel.   b) Frank Lloyd Wright.

3 *The Mona Lisa* was painted by
a) Michelangelo.   b) Leonardo da Vinci.

4 *Madame Butterfly* was written by
a) Giuseppe Verdi.   b) Giacomo Puccini.

10b **Listen and check your answers.** 🎧

Write

11 **Write the answers to Exercise 10a.**

1 The first VW Beetle was made in the 1940s.

Listen and read

12 Listen and note down what Adam (A), Eloisa (E), Dominic (D) and Rachel (R) order.

Rachel Could we have a table for seven, please?
Waiter Seven? Have you booked?
Becky No, we haven't.
Waiter Well, let's see. You can have the table over there.

What would you like to start with?

I'd like melon, please

Menu

Starters

Tomato soup _A_

Melon

Prawn salad

Main courses

Chicken in sauce with rice

Steak and chips

Grilled salmon

Desserts

Sticky toffee pudding

Fruit salad

Ice cream

Talk time

13 **Take turns to order from the menu above.**

Waiter Are you ready to order?
You Yes.
Waiter What would you like?
You I'd like .... to start with.
Waiter And to follow?
You I'd like ....
Waiter Thank you.

Waiter Would you like a dessert?
You Yes, please. I'd like ....

 Listen

14 **What do they think of the food? Look at the menu again. Put a tick (✓) next to the things they like and a cross (✗) next to the things they don't like.**

 Extra!

15 **Imagine you and your partner are eating the food you ordered. Ask each other about the food.**

16 **Listen and read.**

Becky	Are you sad to be going home?
Eloisa	Yes, I am. I'll miss you all.
Rachel	What do you think of Cambridge, Tommaso? Have you had a good time?
Tommaso	It's been great.
Adam	Will you come back?
Tommaso	I'd like to.
Eloisa	Me too! Are you going to visit me in Mexico, Adam?
Becky	What's this? When are you going to Mexico?
Eddie	Can I come too?
Eloisa	You can all come.

Grammar focus

Reported questions

Do you remember the rules about changing tenses in reported speech? Look back at page 108. In reported questions you must also change the word order.

Question-word questions

When are you going to visit me in Mexico?

Eloisa asked Adam when **he was** going to visit her in Mexico. (NOT: Eloisa asked Adam when ~~was he~~ going to visit her in Mexico.)

Yes/No questions

When you report *Yes/No* questions you need to use *if*.

Are you sad to be going home?

Becky asked Eloisa **if** she was sad to be going home.

We don't use the auxiliary *do/does* or *did* in reported questions:

What do you think of Cambridge, Tommaso?

Rachel asked Tommaso what he thought of Cambridge.

Grammar practice

17 **Without looking at the dialogue, try to remember the questions they asked.**

1 Eloisa asked Adam if he was going to visit her in Mexico. *Are you going to visit me in Mexico, Adam?*
2 Becky asked Eloisa if she was sad to be going home.
3 Adam asked Tommaso if he would come back.
4 Becky asked Adam when he was going to Mexico.
5 Eddie asked Eloisa if he could come too.

Pronunciation

Weak forms of prepositions

18 **Listen to each word. Then listen to the same word in a sentence. Practise the sentences with a partner.**

1	from	I'm **from** Milan.
2	for	We've been waiting here **for** ages.
3	at	The next tour will begin **at** 11 o'clock.
4	of	The bridge in front **of** us is called the Wooden Bridge.
5	to	I'm going **to** have the sticky toffee pudding.

Portfolio

19 **Order a meal in a restaurant. Go to page 132.**

Listen and read

1 **Listen and read.**

The boy who sailed across the Atlantic

Sebastian Clover, 15, the youngest person to sail solo across the Atlantic

Sunday

I woke up and noticed that I was only 13 miles from the end of my journey. If I'd slept any longer, I'd have hit the rocks and my boat would have sunk. At first light, I sailed into Antigua harbour. I jumped off the boat and almost fell over. It felt strange being on land.

Monday

I was invited to the Antigua Yacht Club with Mum and Dad. I was also invited to come back for the sailing week later this year. Great!

Tuesday

I visited Island Academy, a local school, to talk about my adventure. I told them about the dolphins, the flying fish and the killer whales ... and about the loneliness. Later I met the Prime Minister, who presented me with a book on Antigua.

Wednesday

It was my 16th birthday today and it was time to go home. At the airport I was presented with a huge birthday cake which I shared with the other passengers. I looked down from the plane and thought, 'I've been sailing across that ocean for more than three weeks and now it's taking just a few hours to get home.'

Thursday

I arrived home and was welcomed by my friends and by my dog, who was very happy to see me. I had my first decent meal for ages. I've been surviving on cereal, orange juice and tinned food.

Friday

For weeks, I've been looking forward to a hot bath and my own bed. And now I can have both. But I haven't been looking forward to going back to school. I've got lots of work to do before Monday!

Vocabulary

2 **Match the words with their meanings.**

1 .....g...........

1 (rocks)
2 sunk
3 first light
4 harbour
5 killer whales
6 loneliness
7 passengers
8 decent
9 surviving
10 tinned

a) gone down in the water
b) managing to live
c) place where boats sail to
d) the moment when the sun comes up
e) in a metal container
f) travellers on a boat, bus or plane
g) large stones
h) sadness because you have no friends with you
i) very big dangerous mammals that live in the sea
j) of good quality

Comprehension

3 **Put the pictures in the order of events.**

Listen

4 **Which day is it?**

1 Tuesday...

Speak

5 Partner A: Partner B is going to ask you questions about what Sebastian did on Sunday, Monday and Tuesday. Reread his diary entries for those days.

Partner B: Partner A is going to ask you questions about what Sebastian did on Wednesday, Thursday and Friday. Reread his diary entries for those days.

Partner A: Answer Partner B's questions:

B
1 How far was Sebastian from land when he woke up on Sunday?

A 13 miles.

2 When did he sail into Antigua harbour?
3 What was it like being on land again?
4 Where did he go on Monday?
5 Who was with him?
6 Will he go back to Antigua?
7 Where did he go on Tuesday?
8 Why?
9 What did he talk about?
10 Who gave him the book on Antigua?

Partner B: Answer Partner A's questions:

A
1 Why was Wednesday a special day?

B It was Sebastian's birthday.

2 How old was he?
3 What was he given at the airport?
4 What did he do with it?
5 How long did it take him to sail to Antigua?
6 How long did it take him to fly home?
7 When he arrived home, who was there to welcome him?
8 What did he eat and drink when he was on the boat?
9 What was he looking forward to when he was on the boat?
10 When does he go back to school?

Write

6 **Think of a week when you did something unusual or exciting. Write some diary entries for the week.**

A school trip? A holiday? A trip to the seaside or a skiing trip?

10 Culture spot

The most popular food on the planet

1 **Before you read:**

  1 Which of the foods in the pictures can you get in your town?

  2 Which do you like?

  3 Which is your favourite?

Listen and read

2 **Listen and read about the most popular food.**

Vocabulary

3 **Complete the sentences with a correct word from the box.**

wives	size	frozen	~~settlers~~
fishermen	recipe	invented	wrapped

  1 People who make their homes in a new place are called ..settlers...

  2 Your aunts are the ……………...…. of your uncles.

  3 If you know how to make spaghetti Bolognese, you don't need a …………………………..

  4 People whose job is to catch fish are called …………………………………….

  5 You can skate on water when it's ………………….

  6 A present is usually ………………... in pretty paper.

  7 The radio was ………………………. by Marconi.

  8 We've got regular or large pizzas. Which ……………………………... do you want?

Write and speak

4 **Work with a partner. How many questions can you ask and answer about food from around the world? Write your questions first.**

> **A** When was pizza first eaten?

> **B** Pizza was first eaten in about 1800.

> **A** Where was the world's first pizzeria?

First eaten?	About 1800
Where?	Italy

The world's first pizzeria opened in 1830 in Naples. The Pizza Margherita was invented in 1889, in honour of the Italian queen.

Chips

First eaten?	The 1700s
Where?	France

Chips were first made by the wives of poor fishermen. Potatoes were cut to the same size as sprats (small fish), fried and served with the fish to make a bigger meal.

Kebabs

First eaten?   About 4000 BC
Where?   The Middle East

The kebab has become one of the most popular snacks in Britain. It's made of meat, onions and salad, wrapped in a special kind of bread.

Doughnuts

First eaten?   About 1600
Where?   Germany

Doughnuts were invented in Germany but they were taken to America by early European settlers.

Ice cream

First eaten?   1295
Where?   China/Italy

Italy is said to be the home of ice cream, but Marco Polo came back from China with a recipe for a frozen milk pudding which was probably the first ice cream.

Popcorn

First eaten?   More than 500 years ago
Where?   Mexico and South America

Popcorn was discovered when corn (maize) was thrown into the fire. It was eaten by the Incas, the Aztecs and other native Americans. In the twentieth century, it became a snack which was sold in cinemas.

Let's check

Vocabulary check

1   **Complete each sentence with the correct word.**

bowl	~~sweet~~	fork	jug	knife	overdone
napkin	fresh	spoon	delicious	salt	

Pass me the sugar, please. My coffee isn't ..sweet.. enough.

1   This toffee pudding is .... Can I have some more, please?

2   Here's a .... to cut the cake.

3   Here's a .... You don't want to get tomato sauce on your shirt.

4   I'm having soup for lunch so I just need a .... and a ....

5   This fish is really .... My dad caught it this morning.

6   Please pass me the .... and pepper.

7   Can you put a .... of cold water on the table, please?

8   Turn your .... round and round and the spaghetti will stay on it.

9   I'm sorry, I've cooked the pasta for too long. It's ....

Write your score: ..../10

Grammar check

2   **Correct the mistake in each sentence.**

/\ = there's a word missing; X = change one word; ⤷ = change the order of two words; * = you must delete one word.

What you would like to start with? ⤷
 .What would you like to start with?.............

1   She asked me when would I arrive. ⤷

 ....

2   All these photos was taken by my friend Maria. **X**

 ....

3   I have looking for my glasses all day. /\

 ....

4   I asked her she was OK. /\

 ....

5   When was this poem been written? *

 ....

Write your score: ..../5

3   **Choose the correct words for each sentence.**

Last summer I was invited to Turkey ..by.. my pen friend.
   A from   **B** because   **C** by

1   He asked us … ready to order our food.
   A were we   **B** we were   **C** if we were

2   We asked him if we … have the bill.
   A will   **B** could   **C** do

3   How long … you been learning Spanish?
   A were   **B** did   **C** have

4   We asked her where … from.
   A was she   **B** did she   **C** she was

5   We … at the airport by Sandro's parents.
   A met us   **B** were meeting   **C** were met

6   The windows … by someone last night.
   A were broken   **B** was broken   **C** were breaking

7   … been rehearsing for the school play this week.
   A We were   **B** We have   **C** We did

8   I asked him if he … like to go to the beach.
   A would   **B** did   **C** will

9   This necklace … found in a field last week.
   A is found   **B** was   **C** were

10   Eva has … lying in the sun all day.
   A being   **B** been   **C** had

Write your score: ..../10

4   **Make sentences by putting the words in order. Add commas where necessary.**

been / have / doing / knife / that / you / What / with / ?
 What have you been doing with that knife?.......

1   a nice / asked / England / having / her / I / if / in / she / time / was

 ....

2   a / by / nice / really / taught / teacher / We / were

 ....

3   a / cooked / delicious / in / sauce / steak / The / was

 ....

4   asked / been / Greece / He / I'd / if / me / to

 ....

5   because / bedroom / been / tired / her / painting / She's / she's

 ....

Write your score: ..../5

Write your total score: ..../30

How good are you?

★ I'm not very good at this. ★ I'm OK at this. ★ I'm good at this.

Tick (✓) the correct boxes.

		★	★★	★★★
READING I can understand:				
an e-mail about plane times	I'm arriving at Stansted airport on Friday July 9th …			
plans for entertaining a friend from another country	We can show him round.			
an article about a girl who moved from a big town to the country	… in Manchester we used to get dressed up and go bowling … Here we meet at the beach or in the fields …			
a conversation between teenagers and a tour guide	Were girls allowed to study here in those days?			
a general knowledge quiz	Where were the first Olympic Games held?			
a diary of a boy who sailed solo across the Atlantic	I jumped off the boat and almost fell over. It felt strange being on land.			
an article about the most popular food	The Pizza Margherita was invented in 1889 in honour of the Italian queen.			
LISTENING I can understand:				
people's opinions about town and country life	It's quieter and it's easier to relax.			
a phone conversation about what someone has been doing	My mum's been painting my room, so I've been using the living room as my bedroom.			
people's orders in a restaurant	I'd like to start with the tomato soup. And to follow?			
people's comments on the food in a restaurant	I don't really like the chicken. It's too spicy for me.			
WRITING I can write:				
describe the local environment of my school or home	I live in a flat on the fourth floor.			
a paragraph about the advantages and disadvantages of city life or country life	Life in the country is quieter. You can enjoy the views. There aren't many buses so it can be hard to …			
a dialogue in a restaurant	Waiter: Are you ready to order? Customer: Yes, please. I'd like soup to start with.			
diary entries for a week on a trip or holiday	Monday: we arrived at our hotel in the Alps and unpacked.			
questions for a quiz on food	Where was the world's first pizzeria?			
SPEAKING I can:				
role-play a phone conversation with a friend who is coming to my country	OK, so where will I meet you and at what time? I'll be at the airport at 2.15 on Friday.			
compare life in the city and life in the country	I prefer living in the city. It's more exciting.			
talk about what people have been doing	How long have you been learning English?			
ask and answer general knowledge quiz questions	When was the first VW Beetle invented?			
role-play talking about food in a restaurant	The salmon's very fresh. The soup's a bit salty.			
answer questions from memory about an article I have read	Why was Wednesday a special day? It was Sebastian's birthday.			
ask and answer quiz questions about food	When was pizza first eaten? Pizza was first eaten in about 1800.			

Vocabulary groups

Write three more words in each vocabulary group.

Streets in town	bus stop	roundabout	....	....	....
Features of the country	stream	bridge	....	....	....
Things on the table	knife	salt	....	....	....
Commenting on food	delicious	nice	....	....	....

1 **Answer the questions.**

1 Where did you go?
2 Who did you go with?
3 What time did you leave home?
4 Did you stop on the way?
5 What time did you arrive?

6 What did you do?
7 What was it like?
8 Did you buy anything?
9 Did you have a meal? What did you have?
10 Did you have a good time?

2 **Write an e-mail to a friend describing a trip you went on recently.**
Use your answers to the questions and Gemma's e-mail to help you.

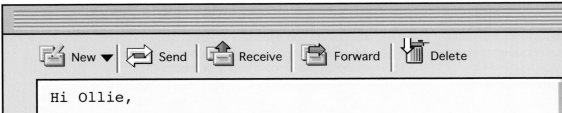 New ▼ | Send | Receive | Forward | Delete

Hi Ollie,

How are you? Hope you're OK.

Guess what? I went to a water park last week with my friend Piers and his family. We left home at 8 o'clock in the morning and we stopped for breakfast on the way. We arrived at 10 o'clock when the park was just opening. We went on all the slides. Some of them were really scary but they were great. We bought a photo of Piers and me on the water chute. We were laughing and we got really wet. We had a big sandwich and a drink for lunch. After lunch, we went on the best slides again. We had a great time!

Write soon,

Love

Gemma

(1) **Record one of the scenes from Cinderella.**

1 Turn to pages 48–49 and choose your scene.

2 How many people are in the scene? Choose a person for each part.

3 In groups, listen to the scene. Do you need any sound effects?
How are you going to make them?

4 Find the things you need for the sound effects.

5 Listen to the scene again, paying attention to how the characters say the lines.

6 Read the scene in groups.

7 Learn your own part.

8 Practise the scene in groups without looking at the book.

9 Practise the scene again with the sound effects.

10 Record the scene.

(1) **Make a list of four people you know and the jobs they do. Ask your teacher for the words you don't know.**

My dad works in a restaurant.

My mum is a doctor.

1 ....

2 ....

3 ....

4 ....

(2) **Ask the people you wrote about in Exercise 1 the following questions.**

1 Do you enjoy working in a shop/in an office?

2 Do you enjoy working on your own/with other people?

3 Do you mind working late?

4 Do you hope to be famous one day?

5 Do you enjoy solving problems?

6 Do you travel in your job?

7 Do you speak any foreign languages?

8 What do you like about your job?

9 What do you dislike about your job?

10 Are there any other jobs you would like to do?

(3) **Write a short paragraph about each person.**

My aunt works in a college. She enjoys

working with other people. She enjoys

solving problems but she doesn't like

working late.

I'd buy a house with a swimming pool for my family.

(1) **Write about 50 words beginning: 'If I were a millionaire ...'.**

Use some of these verbs in your answer.

get	buy	give	go
visit	travel	help	see
stay	spend	have	take

If I were a millionaire...

I'd take my family on holiday. We'd go to ....
Florida. We'd stay in a nice hotel and we'd visit ......
Disneyland. After that we'd go to Australia to ....
see some kangaroos and koala bears. And I'd like ...
to go surfing. Then we'd go to Antarctica to see ....
polar bears and penguins. My sister wouldn't like ...
it there because it's cold, so after that we'd go ....
to Greece for a holiday in the sun.

I'd get my mum a nice new car.

1 **Work in groups of four or five. One of you is a waiter at the Riverside Restaurant. The others want to have dinner there. Write a dialogue.**

Customer 1	Ask for a table. *Could we have a table for (four), please?*
Waiter	Ask if they've booked.
Customer 1	Respond.
Waiter	Ask if the customers are ready to order.
Customers	Tell the waiter what you would like (starters, main courses and side dishes). (The waiter writes down the orders.)
Waiter	Ask the customers if they are enjoying their meal.
Customers	Comment on the meal.
Waiter	Ask if the customers would like dessert.
Customers	Tell the waiter what you would like for dessert. (The waiter writes down the orders.)
Customers	Comment on the desserts.
Customers	Ask if you could have the bill.

The Riverside Restaurant

Starters
Melon with Parma ham
Vegetable soup
Avocado pear with prawns

Main courses
Fillet steak
Roast chicken
Grilled salmon
Mushroom, spinach and cheese tart

Side dishes
Roast potatoes
Mashed potatoes
Boiled new potatoes
Chips
Broccoli, peas and carrots
Mixed salad
Green salad

Desserts
Apple crumble
(served with cream, ice cream or custard)
Strawberry meringue
Chocolate mousse
Fruit salad

2a **Practise your dialogue with the script.**

2b **Practise your dialogue without the script.**

3 **Record your dialogue.**

Sing a song
I Can See Clearly Now
by Johnny Nash

bad   blue
clouds   day
now   rain
rainbow   see

1 Put the words in the correct places in the song.

1 I can .....see......... (1) clearly now, the .... (2) has gone,
I can see all obstacles in my way.
Gone are the dark .... (3) that had me blind.
It's gonna be a bright (bright), bright (bright)
Sun-shiny .... (4)

2 I think I can make it .... (5), the pain has gone
All of the .... (6) feelings have disappeared.
Here is the .... (7) I've been praying for.
It's gonna be a bright (bright), bright (bright)
Sun-shiny day.

Look all around, there's nothing but .... (8) skies
Look straight ahead, nothing but blue skies.

(Repeat verse 1)

gonna = going to

2 Then listen and check. 🎧

Sing a song

1 Fill in the gaps in the first verse and the chorus.

Love at First Sight
by Kylie Minogue

Thought that I was going (**1**) ...crazy......
Just having one of those days yeah
Didn't know what to do
Then there was (**2**) ....

And everything went from wrong to (**3**) ....
And the stars came out and filled up the (**4**)
....
The music you were playing really blew my mind
It was love at first sight

Chorus
  'Cause baby when I heard you
  For the first time I (**5**) ....
  We were meant to be as one

I was tired of running out of luck
Thinking about giving up, yeah
Didn't know what to do
Then there was you

And everything went from wrong to right
And the stars came out and filled up the sky
The music you were playing really blew my mind
It was love at first sight

Chorus (twice)

And everything went from wrong to right
And the stars came out and filled up the sky
The music you were playing really blew my mind
It was love at first sight

Love at first sight
Ooh love at first sight
Love...ooh it was love it was love
at first sight

Chorus (twice)

It was love it was love it was love it was love
Ooh, it was love it was love it was love it was love
Ooh......

2 Listen to the song and check your answers.

3 Read these sentences from the song. Which ones describe positive experiences? Which ones describe negative experiences? Mark them with + (positive) or - (negative).

1 I was just having one of those days.

2 I didn't know what to do.

3 Everything went from wrong to right.

4 The music you were playing really blew my mind.

5 It was love at first sight.

6 I was tired of running out of luck.

7 I was thinking about giving up.

Irregular verbs

Infinitive	Past simple	Past participle
be	was/were	been
become	became	become
begin	began	begun
bite	bit	bitten
break	broke	broken
bring	brought	brought
build	built	built
burn	burned/burnt	burned/burnt
buy	bought	bought
catch	caught	caught
choose	chose	chosen
come	came	come
cost	cost	cost
cut	cut	cut
do	did	done
drink	drank	drunk
drive	drove	driven
eat	ate	eaten
fall	fell	fallen
feel	felt	felt
find	found	found
fly	flew	flown
forget	forgot	forgotten
get	got	got
give	gave	given
go	went	been/gone
have	had	had
hear	heard	heard
hit	hit	hit
hold	held	held
keep	kept	kept
know	knew	known
learn	learned/learnt	learned/learnt
leave	left	left
let	let	let

Infinitive	Past simple	Past participle
lose	lost	lost
make	made	made
meet	met	met
pay	paid	paid
put	put	put
read /riːd/	read /red/	read /red/
ride	rode	ridden
ring	rang	rung
run	ran	run
say	said	said
see	saw	seen
send	sent	sent
shoot	shot	shot
shut	shut	shut
sing	sang	sung
sink	sank	sunk
sit	sat	sat
sleep	slept	slept
speak	spoke	spoken
spend	spent	spent
stand	stood	stood
swim	swam	swum
swing	swung	swung
take	took	taken
teach	taught	taught
tell	told	told
think	thought	thought
throw	threw	thrown
understand	understood	understood
wake up	woke up	woken up
wear	wore	worn
win	won	won
write	wrote	written

A

a bit	/ə ˈbɪt/
ability	/əˈbɪlɪtɪ/
able (be able)	/ˈeɪbl/ /biː ˈeɪbl/
able-bodied	/ˈeɪbl ˌbɒdɪd/
above	/əˈbʌv/
accent	/ˈæksənt/
accept	/əkˈsept/
access (internet access)	/ˈækses/ /ˈɪntənet ækses/
accident	/ˈæksɪdənt/
accommodate	/əˈkɒmədeɪt/
accommodation	/əˌkɒməˈdeɪʃn/
ache (I've got stomach ache.)	/eɪk/ /aɪv ɡɒt ˈstʌmək eɪk/
achieve	/əˈtʃiːv/
act	/ækt/
acting	/ˈæktɪŋ/
action	/ˈækʃn/
activity	/ækˈtɪvɪtɪ/
actor	/ˈæktə(r)/
actress	/ˈæktrəs/
actually	/ˈæktʃʊəlɪ/
admire	/ədˈmaɪə(r)/
adore	/əˈdɔː(r)/
adult	/ˈædʌlt/
adventure	/ədˈventʃə(r)/
aeroplane	/ˈeərəpleɪn/
affect	/əˈfekt/
after	/ˈɑːftə(r)/
again	/əˈɡen/
against	/əˈɡenst/
ages (for ages)	/ˈeɪdʒɪz/ /fə(r) ˈeɪdʒɪz/
ago	/əˈɡəʊ/
agree	/əˈɡriː/
ahead of	/əˈhed əv/
air conditioning	/ˈeə kənˈdɪʃnɪŋ/
airline	/ˈeəlaɪn/
airport	/ˈeəpɔːt/
alcohol	/ˈælkəhɒl/
allow	/əˈlaʊ/
almost	/ˈɔːlməʊst/
alone	/əˈləʊn/
along with	/əˈlɒŋ wɪð/
already	/ɔːlˈredɪ/
altogether	/ˌɔːltəˈɡeðə(r)/
ambulance	/ˈæmbjʊləns/
amount	/əˈmaʊnt/
ankle	/ˈæŋkl/
anybody	/ˈenɪbɒdɪ/
anyone	/ˈenɪwʌn/
anyone else	/ˈenɪwʌn ˈels/
anyway	/ˈenɪweɪ/
apart from	/əˈpɑːt frəm/
appear	/əˈpɪə(r)/
apply	/əˈplaɪ/
archaeologist	/ˌɑːkɪˈɒlədʒɪst/
architect	/ˈɑːkɪtekt/
Arctic Circle	/ˌɑːktɪk ˈsɜːkl/
Arm	/ɑːm/
around (swim around)	/əˈraʊnd/ /swɪm əˈraʊnd/
around here	/əˈraʊnd hɪə(r)/
(you aren't from around here)	/juː ɑːnt frəm əˈraʊnd hɪə(r)/
arrange	/əˈreɪndʒ/
arrivals	/əˈraɪvlz/
arrive	/əˈraɪv/
artist	/ˈɑːtɪst/
ask	/ɑːsk/
as soon as	/əz ˈsuːn əz/
asthma	/ˈæsmə/
at first	/ət ˈfɜːst/
at last	/ət ˈlɑːst/
at least	/ət ˈliːst/
ate ◀ eat	/eɪt, iːt/
Atlantic	/ətˈlæntɪk/
atmosphere	/ˈætməsfɪə/
attention (centre of attention)	/əˈtenʃn/ /sentə(r) əv əˈtenʃn/
audience	/ˈɔːdɪəns/
aunt	/ɑːnt/
available	/əˈveɪləbl/
Aztec	/ˈæztek/

B

baby	/ˈbeɪbɪ/
back (adv.)	/bæk/
back in Manchester	/bæk ɪn ˈmæntʃɪstə(r)/
back (n.)	/bæk/
bacon	/ˈbeɪkn/
baggage reclaim	/ˈbæɡɪdʒ riːkleɪm/
baggy	/ˈbæɡɪ/
bagpipes	/ˈbæɡpaɪps/
balcony	/ˈbælkənɪ/

ball	/bɔːl/
ballet	/ˈbæleɪ/
ban	/bæn/
banjo	/ˈbændʒəʊ/
bank	/bæŋk/
bank manager	/ˈbæŋk mænɪdʒə(r)/
bar	/bɑː(r)/
barbecue	/ˈbɑːbəkjuː/
barn	/bɑːn/
baseball field	/ˈbeɪsbɔːl fiːld/
basement	/ˈbeɪsmənt/
bat	/bæt/
batter (n)	/bæt (r)/
battery	/ˈbætərɪ/
be back by	/biː ˈbæk baɪ/
bear	/beə(r)/
became ◀ become	/bɪˈkeɪm/
because of	/bɪˈkʌz əv/
been; be; go	/biːn/
beetle	/ˈbiːtl/
beginning	/bɪˈɡɪnɪŋ/
bell	/bel/
belong	/bɪˈlɒŋ/
beside	/bɪˈsaɪd/
best (he's doing his best)	/best/ /hiːz duːɪŋ hɪz ˈbest/
better	/ˈbetə(r)/
between	/bɪˈtwiːn/
bird	/bɜːd/
bit (a bit)	/bɪt/ /ə ˈbɪt/
bizarre	/bɪˈzɑː(r)/
bleeding (You're bleeding)	/ˈbliːdɪŋ/ /jɔː ˈbliːdɪŋ/
blew	/bluː/
blind (adj)	/blaɪnd/
blinds	/blaɪndz/
block of flats	/blɒk əv ˈflæts/
board	/bɔːd/
boarder	/ˈbɔːdə(r)/
boarding school	/ˈbɔːdɪŋ skuːl/
boat	/bəʊt/
boil (v.)	/bɔɪl/
bones	/bəʊnz/
book	/bʊk/
boots	/buːts/
boring	/ˈbɔːrɪŋ/
born (was born)	/bɔːn/ /wəz ˈbɔːn/
borrow	/ˈbɒrəʊ/
both ... and	/bəʊθ... ənd/
bought ◀ buy	/bɔːt, baɪ/
bowl	/bəʊl/
bowling (go bowling)	/ˈbəʊlɪŋ/ /ɡəʊ ˈbəʊlɪŋ/
boyfriend	/ˈbɔɪfrend/
branch	/brɑːntʃ/
break (v.)	/breɪk/
breathe	/briːð/
breathing	/ˈbriːðɪŋ/
bridge	/brɪdʒ/
bring	/brɪŋ/
broken ◀ break	/ˈbrəʊkn, breɪk/
brought ▶	
I've brought a friend along.	/ˌaɪv brɔːt ə ˈfrend əlɒŋ/
brush	/brʌʃ/
Brussels	/ˈbrʌsəlz/
building	/ˈbɪldɪŋ/
built ◀ build	/bɪlt, bɪld/
bull	/bʊl/
burned down	/bɜːnd ˈdaʊn/
burnt ◀ burn	/bɜːnt, bɜːn/
bus stop	/ˈbʌs stɒp/
buy	/baɪ/
By the way, ...	/baɪ ðə ˈweɪ/

C

cab	/kæb/
cake	/keɪk/
call (n.)	/kɔːl/
call (v.)	/kɔːl/
came from	/keɪm frəm/
canal	/kəˈnæl/
cancel	/ˈkænsl/
candle	/ˈkændl/
cap (baseball cap)	/kæp/ /ˈbeɪsbɔːl kæp/
captain	/ˈkæptɪn/
caravan	/ˈkærəvæn/
career	/kəˈrɪə(r)/
careful	/ˈkeəfl/
carpet	/ˈkɑːpɪt/
carry	/ˈkærɪ/
carry on (v.)	/ˌkærɪ ˈɒn/
cast	/kɑːst/
catch	/kætʃ/

cattery	/ˈkætəri/
caught ◄ catch	/kɔːt, kætʃ/
celebrate	/ˈseləbreɪt/
central heating	/ˌsentrəl ˈhiːtɪŋ/
central heating control	/ˌsentrəl ˈhiːtɪŋ kənˈtrəʊl/
century	/ˈsentʃəri/
cereal	/ˈsɪəriəl/
ceremony	/ˈserəməni/
chain	/tʃeɪn/
chance	/tʃɑːns/
chandelier	/ʃændəˈlɪə(r)/
change	/tʃeɪndʒ/
chapel	/ˈtʃæpl/
character (main character)	/ˈkærɪktə(r) /meɪn ˈkærɪktə(r)/
charge (free of charge)	/tʃɑːdʒ/ /friː əv ˈtʃɑːdʒ/
chase	/tʃeɪs/
check	/tʃek/
check in	/tʃek ˈɪn/
check-in desk	/ˈtʃekɪn desk/
chef	/ʃef/
chicken	/ˈtʃɪkɪn/
Chinese Whispers	/tʃaɪniːz ˈwɪspəz/
chips	/tʃɪps/
chocolate (hot chocolate)	/ˈtʃɒklət/ /hɒt ˈtʃɒklət/
choose	/tʃuːz/
chores	/tʃɔːz/
Church of England	/ˌtʃɜːtʃ əv ˈɪŋglənd/
claws	/klɔːz/
clean up	/kliːn ˈʌp/
climb	/klaɪm/
close to	/kləʊs tə/
closer	/ˈkləʊsə(r)/
clothes	/kləʊðz/
club (golf club)	/klʌb/ /gɒlf klʌb/
coach	/kəʊtʃ/
cocoa beans	/ˈkəʊkəʊ biːnz/
coconut	/ˈkəʊkənʌt/
coconut palm	/ˈkəʊkənʌt pɑːm/
coffee bar	/ˈkɒfi bɑː(r)/
coffee machine	/ˈkɒfi məʃiːn/
coin	/kɔɪn/
cold (I've got a cold)	/kəʊld/ /aɪv gɒt ə ˈkəʊld/
collect	/kəˈlekt/
colour	/ˈkʌlə(r)/
colourful	/ˈkʌləfʊl/
comb	/kəʊm/
come back	/kʌm ˈbæk/
come off	/kʌm ˈɒf/
come on	/kʌm ˈɒn/
comedy	/ˈkɒmədi/
communication	/kəˌmjuːnɪˈkeɪʃn/
community college	/kəˈmjuːnɪti kɒlɪdʒ/
competition	/ˌkɒmpəˈtɪʃn/
competitive	/kəmˈpetɪtɪv/
complain	/kəmˈpleɪn/
complete	/kəmˈpliːt/
complicated	/ˈkɒmplɪkeɪtɪd/
comprehensive school	/ˌkɒmprɪˈhensɪv skuːl/
concert	/ˈkɒnsət/
cone	/kəʊn/
Congratulations!	/kənˌgrætʃəˈleɪʃnz/
container	/kənˈteɪnə(r)/
conversation	/ˌkɒnvəˈseɪʃn/
cook	/kʊk/
cooker	/ˈkʊkə(r)/
cool	/kuːl/
corn	/kɔːn/
cost	/kɒst/
costume (swimming costume)	/ˈkɒstʃuːm/ /ˈswɪmɪŋ kɒstʃuːm/
cough (I've got a cough)	/kɒf/ /aɪv gɒt ə ˈkɒf/
could	/kʊd/
countryside	/ˈkʌntrɪsaɪd/
courage	/ˈkʌrɪdʒ/
course	/kɔːs/
court (basketball/	/kɔːt/ /bɑːskɪtbɔːl,
volleyball/tennis court)	vɒlibɔːl, tenɪs kɔːt/
cousin	/ˈkʌzn/
cover	/ˈkʌvə(r)/
cow	/kaʊ/
cowshed	/ˈkaʊʃed/
cried ◄ cry	/kraɪd, kraɪ/
criminal	/ˈkrɪmɪnəl/
criticise	/ˈkrɪtɪsaɪz/
crocodile	/ˈkrɒkədaɪl/
crop	/krɒp/
cross (get cross)	/krɒs/ /get ˈkrɒs/
crossroads	/ˈkrɒsrəʊdz/
cruel	/ˈkruːəl/
crystal	/ˈkrɪstl/
culture	/ˈkʌltʃə(r)/
cup	/kʌp/

curious	/ˈkjʊəriəs/
curry	/ˈkʌri/
cushion	/ˈkʊʃn/
cut	/kʌt/
cute	/kjuːt/
cycle	/ˈsaɪkl/
cycle lane	/ˈsaɪkl leɪn/
cyclist	/ˈsaɪklɪst/

D

dance classes	/dɑːns klɑːsɪz/
danger	/ˈdeɪndʒə(r)/
dangerous	/ˈdeɪndʒərəs/
date	/deɪt/
daughter	/ˈdɔːtə(r)/
deaf	/def/
dear (**Oh dear!**)	/dɪə(r)/ /əʊ ˈdɪə(r)/
death	/deθ/
decent	/ˈdiːsənt/
decide	/dɪˈsaɪd/
definitely	/ˈdefɪnɪtli/
delay	/dɪˈleɪ/
delicious	/dɪˈlɪʃəs/
deliver	/dɪˈlɪvə(r)/
demolish	/dɪˈmɒlɪʃ/
dentist	/ˈdentɪst/
departures	/dɪˈpɑːtʃəz/
deposit	/dɪˈpɒzɪt/
design	/dɪˈzaɪn/
dessert spoon	/dɪˈzɜːt spuːn/
detached	/dɪˈtætʃt/
determined	/dɪˈtɜːmɪnd/
dial	/ˈdaɪəl/
die	/daɪ/
different	/ˈdɪfrənt/
directory enquiries	/daɪˌrektrɪ ɪŋˈkwaɪəriːz/
dirty (get dirty)	/ˈdɜːti/ /get ˈdɜːti/
disabled	/dɪsˈeɪbld/
disadvantage	/ˌdɪsədˈvɑːntɪdʒ/
disappointed	/ˌdɪsəˈpɔɪntɪd/
disco	/ˈdɪskəʊ/
discover	/dɪsˈkʌvə(r)/
disgrace	/dɪsˈgreɪs/
disgraceful	/dɪsˈgreɪsfl/
dishes	/ˈdɪʃɪz/
dishwasher	/ˈdɪʃwɒʃə(r)/
dizzy (I feel dizzy)	/ˈdɪzi/ /aɪ fiːl ˈdɪzi/
doctor	/ˈdɒktə(r)/
dog sledding	/dɒg sledɪŋ/
doll	/dɒl/
dolphin	/ˈdɒlfɪn/
done ◄ do	/dʌn, duː/
donkey	/ˈdɒŋki/
dorm	/dɔːm/
double room	/dʌbl ˈruːm/
doughnut	/ˈdəʊnʌt/
down (get down)	/daʊn/ /get ˈdaʊn/
down (just down the road)	/daʊn/ /dʒʌst daʊn ðə ˈrəʊd/
drama	/ˈdrɑːmə/
drawing	/ˈdrɔːɪŋ/
dream	/driːm/
dresscode	/dres/
dress	/dres/
dress rehearsal	/dres rɪˈhɜːsl/
dressed (get dressed up)	/drest/ /get drest ˈʌp/
drive	/draɪv/
duck	/dʌk/
dump (a bit of a dump)	/dʌmp/ /ə bɪt əv ə ˈdʌmp/
during	/ˈdjʊəriŋ/
DVD player	/diː viː diː pleɪə(r)/
dye (v)	/daɪ/

E

each other	/iːtʃ ˈʌðə(r)/
early	/ˈɜːli/
earn	/ɜːn/
eaten ◄ eat	/iːtn, iːt/
education	/edʒʊˈkeɪʃn/
effort	/ˈefət/
else (anyone else)	/els/ /eniwʌn ˈels/
e-mail	/ˈiːmeɪl/
embarrassing	/ɪmˈbærəsɪŋ/
emerald	/ˈemərəld/
emigrate	/ˈemɪgreɪt/
encourage	/ɪnˈkʌrɪdʒ/
end	/end/
end of term	/end əv ˈtɜːm/
engineer	/endʒɪˈnɪə(r)/
enough	/ɪˈnʌf/
ensuite	/ɒnˈswiːt/

entertainment	/ˌentəˈteɪnmənt/
entirely	/ɪnˈtaɪəlɪ/
entrance	/ˈentrəns/
envelope	/ˈenvələʊp/
equal	/ˈiːkwəl/
equipment	/ɪˈkwɪpmənt/
escalator	/ˈeskəleɪtə(r)/
especially	/ɪˈspeʃlɪ/
estate (housing estate)	/ɪˈsteɪt/ /ˈhaʊzɪŋ ɪsteɪt/
European	/ˌjʊərəˈpɪən/
eve (New Year's Eve)	/iːv/ /njuː jɪəz ˈiːv/
even (adj.)	/ˈiːvn/
event	/ɪˈvent/
ever	/ˈevə(r)/
everybody	/ˈevrɪbɒdɪ/
everybody else	/ˈevrɪbɒdɪ ˈels/
everyone	/ˈevrɪwʌn/
everything	/ˈevrɪθɪŋ/
everywhere	/ˈevrɪweə(r)/
exactly	/ɪgˈzæktlɪ/
except	/ɪkˈsept/
exciting	/ɪkˈsaɪtɪŋ/
exit	/ˈeksɪt/
expect	/ɪkˈspekt/
expensive	/ɪkˈspensɪv/
experiment	/ɪkˈsperɪmənt/
explain	/ɪkˈspleɪn/
explore	/ɪkˈsplɔː(r)/
expression	/ɪkˈspreʃn/

F

factory	/ˈfæktərɪ/
fail	/feɪl/
fair (it's not fair)	/feə(r)/ /ɪts nɒt ˈfeə(r)/
fairly	/ˈfeəlɪ/
fairy godmother	/ˈfeərɪ ˈgɒdmʌðə(r)/
fallen in	/ˈfɔːln ˈɪn/
fallen off (fall off)	/ˈfɔːln ˈɒf/
fame	/feɪm/
fancy	/ˈfænsɪ/
fancy dress party	/ˈfænsɪ ˈdres pɑːtɪ/
fantastic	/fænˈtæstɪk/
farm	/fɑːm/
farmer	/ˈfɑːmə(r)/
farmhouse	/ˈfɑːmhaʊs/
fashion	/ˈfæʃn/
faster	/ˈfɑːstə(r)/
fault (it's my fault)	/fɒlt/ /ɪts ˈmaɪ fɒlt/
feed	/fiːd/
feet	/fiːt/
fell off	/fel ˈɒf/
fell over	/fel ˈəʊvə(r)/
fence	/fens/
ferry	/ˈferɪ/
festival	/ˈfestɪvl/
few (a few)	/fjuː/ /ə ˈfjuː/
fiddle	/ˈfɪdl/
field	/fiːld/
filming	/ˈfɪlmɪŋ/
final	/ˈfaɪnəl/
finals	/ˈfaɪnəlz/
find out	/faɪnd ˈaʊt/
fine	/faɪn/
fire	/ˈfaɪə(r)/
firefighter	/ˈfaɪəfaɪtə(r)/
first (at first)	/fɜːst/ /ət ˈfɜːst/
fish	/fɪʃ/
fish cake	/ˈfɪʃ keɪk/
fishermen	/ˈfɪʃəmən/
fit (adj.) (keep fit)	/fɪt/ /kiːp fɪt/
fit (v.)	/fɪt/
flag	/flæg/
flamingo	/fləˈmɪŋgəʊ/
flavour (n.)	/ˈfleɪvə(r)/
flight	/flaɪt/
flight attendant	/ˈflaɪt ətendənt/
floor	/flɔː(r)/
flying fish	/ˈflaɪɪŋ ˈfɪʃ/
folk music	/ˈfəʊk mjuːzɪk/
follow ▶ And to follow, ...	/ənd tə ˈfɒləʊ .../
food processor	/ˈfuːd prəʊsesə(r)/
footpath	/ˈfʊtpɑːθ/
for ages	/fə(r) ˈeɪdʒɪz/
foreign	/ˈfɒrɪn/
fork	/fɔːk/
forward ▶ I'm looking forward to seeing you.	/aɪm lʊkɪŋ fɔːwəd tə ˈsiːɪŋ juː/
found ◀ find	/faʊnd, faɪnd/
foundation stone	/faʊnˈdeɪʃn stəʊn/
fox	/fɒks/

free	/friː/
free of charge	/friː əv ˈtʃɑːdʒ/
freedom	/ˈfriːdəm/
freestyle	/ˈfriːstaɪl/
freezer	/ˈfriːzə(r)/
fresh	/freʃ/
fridge	/frɪdʒ/
fried	/fraɪd/
friendly	/ˈfrendlɪ/
friendship	/ˈfrendʃɪp/
frog	/frɒg/
front (in front of)	/frʌnt/ /ɪn ˈfrʌnt əv/
frozen	/ˈfrəʊzn/
full	/fʊl/
full-time	/ˈfʊl taɪm/
funny	/ˈfʌnɪ/
fur	/fɜː(r)/
future	/ˈfjuːtʃə(r)/

G

gallery	/ˈgælərɪ/
game	/geɪm/
garage	/ˈgærɑːʒ, ˈgærɪdʒ/
gate	/geɪt/
geese	/giːs/
generally	/ˈdʒenrəlɪ/
get	/get/
get attention	/get əˈtenʃn/
get better	/get ˈbetə(r)/
get bored of	/get ˈbɔːd əv/
get close to	/get ˈkləʊs tə/
get on well	/get ɒn ˈwel/
get out of	/get ˈaʊt əv/
get ready	/get ˈredɪ/
get there	/get ˈðeə(r)/
ghost	/gəʊst/
girls'	/gɜːlz/
give up	/gɪv ˈʌp/
glacier	/ˈgleɪsɪə(r), ˈglæsɪə(r)/
glass	/glɑːs/
Go ahead.	/gəʊ əˈhed/
go back	/gəʊ ˈbæk/
goal	/gəʊl/
goat	/gəʊt/
goggles (swimming goggles)	/ˈgɒglz/ /ˈswɪmɪŋ gɒglz/
golf course	/ˈgɒlf kɔːs/
gone ◀ go	/gɒn/
Good luck!	/gʊd ˈlʌk/
goose	/guːs/
gorilla	/gəˈrɪlə/
got	/gɒt/
got to	/ˈgɒt tə/
grammar school	/ˈgræmə skuːl/
greasy	/ˈgriːsɪ/
greenhouse	/ˈgriːnhaʊs/
grilled	/grɪld/
group	/gruːp/
grow	/grəʊ/
grow up	/ˌgrəʊ ˈʌp/
Guess what?	/ges ˈwɒt/
guests	/gests/
guide (tour guide)	/gaɪd/ /tʊə gaɪd/
gym	/dʒɪm/

H

had ◀ have	/hæd, hæv/
hair	/heə(r)/
hairdresser	/ˈheədresə(r)/
half-time	/hɑːf ˈtaɪm/
Hallowe'en	/ˌhæləʊˈiːn/
handwritten	/ˈhændrɪtn/
Hang on!	/hæŋ ˈɒn/
hang out with	/hæŋ ˈaʊt wɪð/
happen	/ˈhæpn/
harbour	/ˈhɑːbə(r)/
hard	/hɑːd/
hate	/heɪt/
head	/hed/
hear	/hɪə(r)/
hear from	/hɪə frəm/
heard from	/hɜːd frəm/
heavy metal	/hevɪ ˈmetl/
hedge	/hedʒ/
held (it is held every year)	/held/ /ɪt ɪz held evrɪ ˈjɪə(r)/
hell	/hel/
helmet (cycle helmet)	/ˈhelmɪt/ /ˈsaɪkl helmɪt/
help (I can't help)	/help/ /aɪ kɑːnt ˈhelp/
hen	/hen/
hide	/haɪd/
hill	/hɪl/

hi fi	/ˈhaɪ faɪ/
hire	/ˈhaɪə(r)/
hire out	/ˈhaɪə ˈaʊt/
hold	/həʊld/
hometown	/ˈhəʊmtaʊn/
honey	/ˈhʌni/
honour (in honour of)	/ˈɒnə(r)/ /ɪn ˈɒnə(r) əv/
hope	/həʊp/
horse	/hɔːs/
hot	/hɒt/
hottest ticket	/hɒtɪst ˈtɪkɪt/
houseboat	/ˈhaʊsbəʊt/
How did it go?	/haʊ dɪd ɪt ˈgəʊ/
huge	/hjuːdʒ/
hunger	/ˈhʌŋgə(r)/
hurt	/hɜːt/
husband	/ˈhʌzbənd/
hypnotist	/ˈhɪpnətɪst/

I

I wish I could go	/aɪ ˈwɪʃ aɪ kʊd gəʊ/
I'd like ...	/aɪd laɪk .../
I hope you don't mind.	/aɪ ˌhəʊp juː dəʊnt ˈmaɪnd/
I'm afraid ...	/aɪm əˈfreɪd .../
I'm afraid not.	/aɪm əˈfreɪd ˈnɒt/
ice	/aɪs/
ice-skating	/ˈaɪs skeɪtɪŋ/
ideal	/aɪˈdɪəl/
ill	/ɪl/
illness	/ˈɪlnəs/
immediately	/ɪˈmiːdɪətli/
Incas	/ˈɪŋkəz/
included	/ɪŋˈkluːdɪd/
including	/ɪŋˈkluːdɪŋ/
independence	/ɪndəˈpendəns/
Indian	/ˈɪndɪən/
indoor	/ˈɪndɔː(r)/
information point	/ɪnfəˈmeɪʃn pɔɪnt/
injury	/ˈɪndʒəri/
inside	/ɪnˈsaɪd/
instance (for instance)	/ˈɪnstəns/
instinct	/ˈɪnstɪŋkt/
interested in	/ˈɪntrəstɪd ɪn/
international code	/ɪntəˌnæʃnl ˈkəʊd/
interpreter	/ɪnˈtɜːprɪtə(r)/
into (what are you into?)	/ˈɪntʊ/ /wɒt ə juː ˈɪntuː/
introduce	/ɪntrəˈdjuːs/
invent	/ɪnˈvent/
inventor	/ɪnˈventə(r)/
invitation	/ɪnvɪˈteɪʃn/
invite	/ɪnˈvaɪt/
Ireland	/ˈaɪələnd/
Irish	/ˈaɪrɪʃ/
iron	/ˈaɪən/
isle	/aɪl/
isn't that ...?	/ˈɪznt ðæt .../

J

jealous	/ˈdʒeləs/
jewellery	/ˈdʒuːəlri/
job	/dʒɒb/
join	/dʒɔɪn/
join in	/dʒɔɪn ˈɪn/
joke	/dʒəʊk/
journalist	/ˈdʒɜːnəlɪst/
journey	/ˈdʒɜːni/
judo	/ˈdʒuːdəʊ/
jug	/dʒʌg/
jump	/dʒʌmp/
junior	/ˈdʒuːnɪə(r)/
just right	/dʒʌst ˈraɪt/
just to be sure	/ˌdʒʌst tə biː ˈʃʊə(r)/

K

keen	/kiːn/
keep in touch with	/kiːp ɪn ˈtʌtʃ wɪð/
keep quiet	/kiːp ˈkwaɪət/
kennel	/ˈkenl/
kept	/kept/
kettle	/ˈketl/
key	/kiː/
kick	/kɪk/
kid	/kɪd/
kill	/kɪl/
killer whale	/ˈkɪlə weɪl/
kilt	/kɪlt/
kind	/kaɪnd/
kind of	/ˈkaɪnd əv/
king	/kɪŋ/
kit	/kɪt/

kitchen	/ˈkɪtʃɪn/
kitten	/ˈkɪtn/
knee	/niː/
knife	/naɪf/
knives	/naɪvz/
knock down	/nɒk ˈdaʊn/
knock off	/nɒk ˈɒf/
known ◄ know	/nəʊn, nəʊ/

L

laboratory	/ləˈbɒrətri/
lads	/lædz/
lady	/ˈleɪdi/
lagoon	/ləˈguːn/
laid	/leɪd/
lake	/leɪk/
lamb	/læm/
lamp post	/ˈlæmp pəʊst/
land	/lænd/
landscape	/ˈlænskeɪp/
language	/ˈlæŋgwɪdʒ/
last	/lɑːst/
last (at last)	/lɑːst/ /ət ˈlɑːst/
laugh	/lɑːf/
lazy	/ˈleɪzi/
leave a message	/liːv ə ˈmesɪdʒ/
left	/left/
left (if there's any left)	/left/ /ɪf ðeəz eni ˈleft/
leg	/leg/
lessons	/ˈlesnz/
Let's get started.	/lets get ˈstɑːtɪd/
liberty	/ˈlɪbəti/
library	/ˈlaɪbrəri/
lie	/laɪ/
lie down	/laɪ ˈdaʊn/
life	/laɪf/
lifeguard	/ˈlaɪfgɑːd/
lifetime (of a lifetime)	/ˈlaɪftaɪm/ /ɒv ə ˈlaɪftaɪm/
light (at first light)	/laɪt/ /ət fɜːst ˈlaɪt/
lights (street lights)	/laɪts/ /striːt laɪts/
like (prep.)	/laɪk/
limping	/ˈlɪmpɪŋ/
lines	/laɪnz/
lit	/lɪt/
live	/lɪv/
lively	/ˈlaɪvli/
living area	/ˈlɪvɪŋ eəriə/
loads of	/ˈləʊdz əv/
local	/ˈləʊkl/
location	/ləʊˈkeɪʃn/
lock	/lɒk/
loneliness	/ˈləʊnlinəs/
long (adj.)	/lɒŋ/
long (adv.)	/lɒŋ/
look after	/lʊk ˈɑːftə(r)/
look for	/lʊk fə/
look forward to	/lʊk ˈfɔːwəd tə/
look like	/lʊk laɪk/
look (n.) (have a look)	/lʊk/ /hæv ə ˈlʊk/
look (v.)	/lʊk/
lorry	/ˈlɒri/
lorry driver	/ˈlɒri draɪvə(r)/
lost ► lose	/lɒst, luːz/
lot (one lot of)	/lɒt/
You only get one lot of parents!	/juː ˌəʊnli get ˈwʌn lɒt əv peərənts/
lottery	/ˈlɒtəri/
love from	/ˈlʌv frɒm/
love (n.) (fall in love)	/lʌv/ /fɔːl ɪn ˈlʌv/
loyal	/ˈlɔɪəl/
luckily	/ˈlʌkɪli/
luggage (hand luggage)	/ˈlʌgɪdʒ/
lunch	/lʌntʃ/

M

machine	/məˈʃiːn/
made up with	/meɪd ˈʌp wɪð/
magic	/ˈmædʒɪk/
mainly	/ˈmeɪnli/
maize	/meɪz/
make friends	/meɪk ˈfrendz/
make people laugh	/meɪk piːpl ˈlɑːf/
mammal	/ˈmæml/
manage	/ˈmænɪdʒ/
manager	/ˈmænɪdʒə(r)/
marks (get good marks)	/mɑːks/ /get gʊd ˈmɑːks/
marry	/ˈmæri/
match	/mætʃ/
mate	/meɪt/

May I ...?	/meɪ aɪ .../
maybe	/ˈmeɪbɪ/
meal	/miːl/
mean	/miːn/
meat	/miːt/
medicine	/ˈmedɪsən/
meet	/miːt/
melon	/ˈmelən/
melt	/melt/
member	/ˈmembə(r)/
mention	/ˈmenʃən/
message	/ˈmesɪdʒ/
met	/met/
metal	/ˈmetl/
method	/ˈmeθəd/
microwave	/ˈmaɪkrəʊweɪv/
Middle East	/ˌmɪdl ˈiːst/
midnight	/ˈmɪdnaɪt/
miles	/maɪlz/
milk	/mɪlk/
miniature	/ˈmɪnətʃə(r)/
mind	/maɪnd/
mind ▶ Do you mind if ...?	/duː juː ˈmaɪnd ɪf.../
mind (never)	/maɪnd/ /ˈnevə(r)/
miss	/mɪs/
mixed	/mɪkst/
mixture	/ˈmɪkstʃə(r)/
mobile phone	/ˈməʊbaɪl ˈfəʊn/
money	/ˈmʌnɪ/
more	/mɔː(r)/
motivate	/ˈməʊtɪveɪt/
motorbike	/ˈməʊtəbaɪk/
mountain biking	/ˈmaʊntɪn baɪkɪŋ/
mouse	/maʊs/
mouth	/maʊθ/
move	/muːv/
move in	/muːv ˈɪn/
much better	/mʌtʃ ˈbetə(r)/
much later	/mʌtʃ ˈleɪtə(r)/
muscles	/ˈmʌslz/
musical	/ˈmjuːzɪkl/
musician	/mjuːˈzɪʃn/

N

naïve	/naɪˈiːv/
named after	/ˈneɪmd ɑːftə(r)/
napkin	/ˈnæpkɪn/
Naples	/ˈneɪplz/
native	/ˈneɪtɪv/
naughty	/ˈnɔːtɪ/
near	/nɪə(r)/
nearly	/ˈnɪəlɪ/
need	/niːd/
neighbour	/ˈneɪbə(r)/
neither (neither am I)	/ˈnaɪðə(r)/ /ˈnaɪðə(r) əm ˈaɪ/
nervous	/ˈnɜːvəs/
net	/net/
Never mind.	/ˌnevə ˈmaɪnd/
new	/njuː/
newspaper	/ˈnjuːspeɪpə(r)/
next	/nekst/
next to	/ˈneks tə/
Nice to meet you, too.	/ˌnaɪs tə miːt juː ˈtuː/
Nice to meet you.	/ˌnaɪs tə ˈmiːt juː/
nil	/nɪl/
nobody	/ˈnəʊbɒdɪ/
nor (nor am I)	/nɔː(r)/ /nɔː(r) əm ˈaɪ/
normal	/ˈnɔːml/
Northern Ireland	/ˌnɔːðən ˈaɪələnd/
Not at all.	/ˌnɒt ət ˈɔːl/
notice	/ˈnəʊtɪs/
nowhere	/ˈnəʊweə(r)/
nuisance (be a nuisance)	/ˈnjuːsəns/ /biː ə ˈnjuːsəns/
nurse	/nɜːs/

O

occasion	/əˈkeɪʒn/
ocean	/ˈəʊʃən/
odd	/ɒd/
offer	/ˈɒfə(r)/
office block	/ˈɒfɪs blɒk/
often	/ˈɒfn/
olives	/ˈɒlɪvz/
once	/wʌns/
one (the old one)	/wʌn/ /ðiː ˌəʊld ˈwʌn/
onion	/ˈʌnɪən/
onto	/ˈɒntuː/
open	/ˈəʊpn/
opening	/ˈəʊpnɪŋ/
opera	/ˈɒpərə/

orchestra	/ˈɔːkɪstrə/
original	/əˈrɪdʒənəl/
out (10 out of 10)	/aʊt/ /ten aʊt əv ˈten/
out of (come out of)	/aʊt əv/ /kʌm ˈaʊt əv/
out there	/aʊt ˈðeə/
outdoor	/ˈaʊtdɔː(r)/
outside (adv.)	/aʊtˈsaɪd/
outside (prep.)	/ˈaʊtsaɪd/
oven	/ˈʌvn/
over (all over the floor)	/ˈəʊvə(r)/ /ɔːl ˈəʊvə ðə ˈflɔː(r)/
over (be over)	/ˈəʊvə(r)/ /biː ˈəʊvə(r)/
over (over an hour longer)	/ˈəʊvə(r)/ /ˈəʊvə(r) ən ˈaʊə ˌlɒŋgə(r)/
overcome	/əʊvəˈkʌm/
overdone	/əʊvəˈdʌn/
overlook	/əʊvəˈlʊk/
own (on your own)	/əʊn/ /ɒn jɔː(r) ˈəʊn/
own (adj.)	/əʊn/
own (v.)	/əʊn/
owner	/ˈəʊnə(r)/

P

Pacific Ocean	/pəˌsɪfɪk ˈəʊʃn/
pack	/pæk/
packing (do your packing)	/ˈpækɪŋ/ /duː jə ˈpækɪŋ/
pain	/peɪn/
paint	/peɪnt/
palace	/ˈpælɪs/
pale	/peɪl/
panic ▶ Don't panic!	/dəʊnt ˈpænɪk/
pantomime	/ˈpæntəmaɪm/
paradise	/ˈpærədaɪs/
parent	/ˈpeərənt/
part	/pɑːt/
pass	/pɑːs/
passenger	/ˈpæsɪndʒə(r)/
passion	/ˈpæʃn/
passport control	/ˈpɑːspɔːt kəntrəʊl/
patron saint	/ˈpeɪtrən ˈseɪnt/
pattern	/ˈpætən/
pavement	/ˈpeɪvmənt/
pay	/peɪ/
peaceful	/ˈpiːsfl/
penalty	/ˈpenəltɪ/
pen-friend	/ˈpenfrend/
penny	/ˈpenɪ/
pepper	/ˈpepə(r)/
per	/pə(r)/
perform	/pəˈfɔːm/
performance	/pəˈfɔːməns/
perfume	/ˈpɜːfjuːm/
perhaps	/pəˈhæps/
phone	/fəʊn/
phone call	/ˈfəʊn kɔːl/
photographer	/fəˈtɒgrəfə(r)/
pickled	/ˈpɪkld/
picture	/ˈpɪktʃə(r)/
pie	/paɪ/
piece	/piːs/
pig	/pɪg/
pipes	/paɪps/
pitch (football pitch)	/pɪtʃ/ /ˈfʊtbɔːl pɪtʃ/
pity (n)	/ˈpɪtɪ/
plan (n.) (street plan)	/plæn/ /ˈstriːt plæn/
plan (v.)	/plæn/
plane	/pleɪn/
plant	/plɑːnt/
plate	/pleɪt/
play (n.)	/pleɪ/
play (v.)	/pleɪ/
players	/ˈpleɪəz/
pleased	/pliːzd/
pleases (as it pleases)	/ˈpliːzɪz/ /æz ɪt ˈpliːzɪz/
plot	/plɒt/
poem	/ˈpəʊɪm/
poetry	/ˈpəʊətrɪ/
police	/pəˈliːs/
police officer	/pəˈliːs ɒfɪsə(r)/
police station	/pəˈliːs steɪʃn/
polite	/pəˈlaɪt/
pollution	/pəˈluːʃn/
pond	/pɒnd/
pony	/ˈpəʊnɪ/
pool (swimming pool)	/puːl/ /ˈswɪmɪŋ puːl/
poor	/pʊə(r), pɔː(r)/
popcorn	/ˈpɒpkɔːn/
popular	/ˈpɒpjʊlə(r)/
post	/pəʊst/
post box	/ˈpəʊst bɒks/
post office	/ˈpəʊst ɒfɪs/
postcard	/ˈpəʊstkɑːd/
postcode	/ˈpəʊstkəʊd/

posters	/ˈpəʊstəz/
potato	/pəˈteɪtəʊ/
practise	/ˈpræktɪs/
prawn salad	/prɔːn ˈsæləd/
prefer	/prɪˈfɜː(r)/
present with	/prɪˈzent wɪð/
pretend	/prɪˈtend/
pretty	/ˈprɪtɪ/
priest	/priːst/
prince	/prɪns/
Prince Charming	/prɪns ˈtʃɑːmɪŋ/
prison	/ˈprɪzn/
private school	/praɪvɪt ˈskuːl/
prize	/praɪz/
probably	/ˈprɒbəblɪ/
produce	/prəˈdʒuːs/
professional	/prəˈfeʃnl/
programme	/ˈprəʊɡræm/
promising	/ˈprɒmɪsɪŋ/
proper	/ˈprɒpə(r)/
proud	/praʊd/
PS	/piː ˈes/
publish	/ˈpʌblɪʃ/
punting	/ˈpʌntɪŋ/
pupil	/ˈpjuːpəl/
puppy	/ˈpʌpɪ/
purse	/pɜːs/
push	/pʊʃ/

Q

quality	/ˈkwɒlɪtɪ/
quarter finals	/kɔːtə ˈfaɪnlz/
queen	/kwiːn/
quicker	/ˈkwɪkə(r)/
quite	/kwaɪt/

R

rabbit	/ˈræbɪt/
race	/reɪs/
racecourse	/ˈreɪskɔːs/
racing (Formula 1 racing)	/ˈreɪsɪŋ/
racism	/ˈreɪsɪzm/
racket	/ˈrækɪt/
radiator	/ˈreɪdɪeɪtə(r)/
rain	/reɪn/
ran ◄ run	/ræn/
rang	/ræŋ/
range	/reɪndʒ/
rather than	/ˈrɑːðə ðən/
ready ▶ Are you ready to order?	/ɑː juː ˌredɪ tuː ˈɔːdə(r)/
real	/riːl/
realise	/ˈrɪəlaɪz/
really	/ˈrɪəlɪ/
reason	/ˈriːzn/
rebuilt	/riːˈbɪlt/
receive	/rɪˈsiːv/
recently	/ˈriːsəntlɪ/
receptionist	/rɪˈsepʃnɪst/
recipe	/ˈresɪpɪ/
regional	/ˈriːdʒənl/
regularly	/ˈreɡjələlɪ/
rehearsal	/rɪˈhɜːsl/
rehearse	/rɪˈhɜːs/
reindeer skin	/ˈreɪndɪə skɪn/
relax	/rɪˈlæks/
rent	/rent/
reporter	/rɪˈpɔːtə(r)/
research	/rɪˈsɜːtʃ/
respect	/rɪˈspekt/
rest day	/ˈrest deɪ/
revise	/rɪˈvaɪz/
rice	/raɪs/
rich (the rich)	/rɪtʃ/ /ðə ˈrɪtʃ/
ride a horse	/raɪd ə ˈhɔːs/
right (all right)	/raɪt/ /ɔːl ˈraɪt/
right ▶ Is it all right if ...?	/ɪz ɪt ɔːl raɪt ɪf .../
right ▶ If that's all right.	/ɪf ˌðæts ɔːl ˈraɪt/
rights	/raɪts/
ring	/rɪŋ/
road	/rəʊd/
roast	/rəʊst/
rock	/rɒk/
rock musician	/ˈrɒk mjuːˈzɪʃn/
role model	/ˈrəʊl mɒdl/
romantic	/rəʊˈmæntɪk/
round (get friends round)	/raʊnd/ /ɡet ˈfrendz raʊnd/
roundabout	/ˈraʊndəbaʊt/
route (n)	/ruːt/
royal	/ˈrɔɪəl/

rubbish	/ˈrʌbɪʃ/
rubbish bin	/ˈrʌbɪʃ bɪn/
rucksack	/ˈrʌksæk/
run away	/rʌn əˈweɪ/

S

sad	/sæd/
sadness	/ˈsædnəs/
safe	/seɪf/
safety	/ˈseɪftɪ/
said ◄ say	/sed/
sail	/seɪl/
sail across	/seɪl əˈkrɒs/
sailing	/ˈseɪlɪŋ/
sales assistant	/ˈseɪlz əsɪstənt/
salmon	/ˈsæmən/
salt	/sɒlt/
salty	/ˈsɒltɪ/
same	/seɪm/
sang ◄ sing	/sæŋ/
sauce	/sɔːs/
saucer	/ˈsɔːsə(r)/
save	/seɪv/
saw ◄ see	/sɔː, siː/
scared	/skeəd/
scary	/ˈskeərɪ/
scene	/siːn/
scenery	/ˈsiːnərɪ/
scenic	/ˈsiːnɪk/
scientific	/saɪənˈtɪfɪk/
scientist	/ˈsaɪəntɪst/
scooter	/ˈskuːtə(r)/
score (n.)	/skɔː(r)/
score (v.)	/skɔː(r)/
Scots (the Scots)	/skɒts/ /ðə ˈskɒts/
Scottish	/ˈskɒtɪʃ/
scream	/skriːm/
script	/skrɪpt/
sea	/siː/
seal	/siːl/
seat	/siːt/
secondary school	/ˈsekəndrɪ skuːl/
secret	/ˈsiːkrət/
See if ...	/ˈsiː ɪf .../
See you.	/ˈsiː juː/
See you there.	/siː juː ˈðeə(r)/
seen ◄ see	/siːn, siː/
selective	/sɪˈlektɪv/
semi-detached	/semɪ dɪˈtætʃt/
semi-finals	/semɪ ˈfaɪnlz/
send	/send/
senior	/ˈsiːnɪə(r)/
separate	/ˈsepərət/
series	/ˈsɪərɪːz/
serious (be serious)	/ˈsɪərɪəs/ /bi ˈsɪərɪəs/
serve	/sɜːv/
session (training session)	/seʃn/ /ˈtreɪnɪŋ seʃn/
set (adj.)	/set/
set (n.)	/set/
settler	/ˈsetlə(r)/
several	/ˈsevrəl/
shake	/ʃeɪk/
shallow	/ˈʃæləʊ/
share	/ʃeə(r)/
shed	/ʃed/
sheep	/ʃiːp/
ship	/ʃɪp/
shirt (football shirt)	/ʃɜːt/ /ˈfʊtbɔːl ʃɜːt/
shoe	/ʃuː/
shopping centre	/ˈʃɒpɪŋ sentə(r)/
shorts	/ʃɔːts/
should(n't)	/ˈʃʊdnt/
show (n.)	/ʃəʊ/
show (v.)	/ʃəʊ/
show ▶ We can show you around.	/ˌwiː kən ˈʃəʊ juː əˌraʊnd/
shower (have a shower)	/ˈʃaʊə(r)/ /hæv ə ˈʃaʊə(r)/
Shut up!	/ʃʌt ˈʌp/
Siberian	/saɪˈbɪərɪən/
sick (I feel sick)	/sɪk/ /aɪ fiːl ˈsɪk/
side	/saɪd/
side plate	/ˈsaɪd pleɪt/
sign	/saɪn/
sign language	/ˈsaɪn læŋgwɪdʒ/
signpost	/ˈsaɪnpəʊst/
simple	/ˈsɪmpl/
since	/sɪns/
sincerely (yours sincerely)	/sɪnˈsɪəlɪ/ /jɔːz sɪnˈsɪəlɪ/
singing	/ˈsɪŋɪŋ/
single room	/ˈsɪŋɡl ˈruːm/
sink	/sɪŋk/

size	/saɪz/
skate	/skeɪt/
skirt	/skɜ:t/
sleep	/sli:p/
sleeping bag	/sli:pɪŋ bæg/
sleepover	/sli:pəʊvə(r)/
slept ◄ sleep	/slept, sli:p/
slightly	/slaɪtlɪ/
slowly	/sləʊlɪ/
smart	/smɑ:t/
smile	/smaɪl/
smoking	/sməʊkɪŋ/
snake	/sneɪk/
snow	/snəʊ/
snowboarding	/snəʊbɔ:dɪŋ/
snowmobiling	/snəʊməbi:lɪŋ/
so	/səʊ/
so (and so on)	/səʊ/ /ənd 'səʊ ɒn/
so (so am I)	/səʊ/ /səʊ əm 'aɪ/
soap	/səʊp/
sofa	/səʊfə/
solar-powered	/səʊlə paʊəd/
sold ◄ sell	/səʊld, sel/
solo	/səʊləʊ/
solve	/sɒlv/
somehow	/sʌmhaʊ/
Something's happened.	/sʌmθɪŋz 'hæpnd/
somewhere	/sʌmweə(r)/
son	/sʌn/
sonnet	/sɒnɪt/
soon	/su:n/
sore (I've got a sore throat)	/sɔ:(r)/ /aɪv gɒt ə sɔ: 'θrəʊt/
sort	/sɔ:t/
sound	/saʊnd/
soup spoon	/su:p spu:n/
south	/saʊθ/
southern	/sʌðən/
space	/speɪs/
spare	/speə(r)/
spare time	/speə 'taɪm/
speak	/spi:k/
spend	/spend/
spicy	/spaɪsɪ/
spider	/spaɪdə(r)/
spoken ◄ speak	/spəʊkn, spi:k/
sportsman	/spɔ:tsmən/
sprained	/spreɪnd/
spray	/spreɪ/
squad	/skwɒd/
stable	/steɪbl/
stage	/steɪdʒ/
stage school	/steɪdʒ sku:l/
stall (n)	/stɔ:l/
stamp (v)	/stæmp/
stand	/stænd/
stand up	/stænd 'ʌp/
stand up	/stænd 'ʌp/ /hi: stændz
(he stands up for himself)	ʌp fə hɪm'self/
star (n.)	/stɑ:(r)/
star (v.)	/stɑ:(r)/
state school	/steɪt sku:l/
station	/steɪʃn/
statue	/stætʃu:/
stay (n.)	/steɪ/
stay up	/steɪ 'ʌp/
stay (v.)	/steɪ/
stay with	/steɪ wɪð/
steak	/steɪk/
stick (n)	/stɪk/
stick-thin	/stɪk θɪn/
sticky toffee pudding	/stɪkɪ tɒfɪ 'pʊdɪŋ/
still	/stɪl/
stilts	/stɪlts/
stir	/stɜ:(r)/
steep	/sti:p/
stole ◄ steal	/stəʊl/
stomach	/stʌmək/
stone	/stəʊn/
stood	/stʊd/
stop (bus stop)	/stɒp/ /bʌs stɒp/
stop it	/stɒp ɪt/
stored	/stɔ:d/
story	/stɔ:rɪ/
story-telling	/stɔ:rɪ telɪŋ/
straight	/streɪt/
straight after	/streɪt 'ɑ:ftə(r)/
Straight away	/streɪt ə'weɪ/
stray dog	/streɪ 'dɒg/
stream	/stri:m/
street	/stri:t/
streetwise	/stri:twaɪz/
strict	/strɪkt/
strong	/strɒŋ/
struck ◄ strike	/strʌk/
subject	/sʌbdʒekt/
suburbs	/sʌbɜ:bz/
successful	/sək'sesfʊl/
such as	/sʌtʃ əz/
suffer	/sʌfər/
suit (cold-weather suit)	/su:t/ /kəʊld 'weðə(r) su:t/
summer	/sʌmə(r)/
sunk	/sʌŋk/
sunny (be sunny)	/sʌnɪ/ /bi: sʌnɪ/
superb	/su:'pɜ:b/
support	/sə'pɔ:t/
sure	/ʃʊə(r), ʃɔ:(r)/
surf the net	/sɜ:f ðə 'net/
Surprise, surprise!	/sə'praɪz, sə'praɪz/
surprising	/sə'praɪzɪŋ/
surrounded by	/sə'raʊndɪd baɪ/
survive	/sə'vaɪv/
swap	/swɒp/
sweet	/swi:t/
swept ◄ sweep	/swept/
swim	/swɪm/
swimmer	/swɪmə(r)/
swimming competition	/swɪmɪŋ kɒmpətɪʃn/
swum ◄ swim	/swʌm, swɪm/
syrup	/sɪrəp/

T

take	/teɪk/
take a year out	/teɪk ə jɪə(r) 'aʊt/
take an exam	/teɪk ən ɪg'zæm/
take home	/teɪk 'həʊm/
take photos	/teɪk 'fəʊtəʊz/
talented	/tæləntɪd/
talk	/tɔ:k/
tall	/tɔ:l/
tannoy	/tænɔɪ/
tap	/tæp/
tape	/teɪp/
tasty	/teɪstɪ/
taught ◄ teach	/tɔ:t/
tax	/tæks/
taxi	/tæksɪ/
tea	/ti:/
team	/ti:m/
teapot	/ti:pɒt/
teaspoon	/ti:spu:n/
teeth	/ti:θ/
tell	/tel/
temperature	/temprɪtʃə(r)/
terminal	/tɜ:mɪnl/
terraced house	/terəst haʊs/
test	/test/
text message	/tekst mesɪdʒ/
that	/ðæt/
theatre	/θɪətə(r)/
there	/ðeə(r)/
thing	/θɪŋ/
think (I think so)	/θɪŋk, aɪ 'θɪŋk səʊ/
think about	/θɪŋk əbaʊt/
though	/ðəʊ/
throat	/θrəʊt/
through	/θru:/
thrown	/θrəʊn/
ticket office	/tɪkɪt ɒfɪs/
tidy	/taɪdɪ/
tiger	/taɪgə(r)/
time	/taɪm/
time (for a long time)	/taɪm/ /fə(r) ə 'lɒŋ taɪm/
time (have a good/great) time	/taɪm/ /hæv ə 'gʊd, greɪt 'taɪm/
time (on time)	/taɪm/ /ɒn 'taɪm/
time (three times)	/taɪm/ /θri: taɪmz/
tinned food	/tɪnd fu:d/
tiny	/taɪnɪ/
tired	/taɪəd/
T-junction	/ti: dʒʌŋkʃn/
toaster	/təʊstə(r)/
toe	/təʊ/
together	/tə'geðə(r)/
together with	/tə'geðə wɪð/
told	/təʊld/
tomato	/tə'mɑ:təʊ/
tomorrow	/tə'mɒrəʊ/
tonight	/tə'naɪt/
tonnes	/tʌnz/
too	/tu:/
took ◄ take	/tʊk, teɪk/

took part	/tʊk ˈpɑːt/
took place	/tʊk ˈpleɪs/
tooth	/tuːθ/
top	/tɒp/
touch (n.) (keep in touch with)	/tʌtʃ, kiːp ɪn ˈtʌtʃ wɪð/
touch (v.)	/tʌtʃ/
tough	/tʌf/
tour	/ˈtʊə(r)/
tour (on tour)	/ˈtʊə(r)/ /ɒn ˈtʊə(r)/
tourist guide	/ˈtʊərɪst gaɪd/
tournament	/ˈtɔːnəmənt/
towards	/təˈwɔːdz/
towel	/ˈtaʊəl/
tower block	/ˈtaʊə blɒk/
town	/taʊn/
track (athletics/race)	/træk/ /æθletɪks, reɪs/
tracksuit	/ˈtræksuːt/
tradition	/trəˈdɪʃn/
traffic	/ˈtræfɪk/
traffic lights	/ˈtræfɪk laɪts/
train	/treɪn/
trainers	/ˈtreɪnəz/
training	/ˈtreɪnɪŋ/
translator	/trænzˈleɪtə(r)/
transport	/ˈtrænzpɔːt/
travel	/ˈtrævl/
traveller	/ˈtrævlə(r)/
treat	/triːt/
tribute	/ˈtrɪbjuːt/
trick (n)	/trɪk/
trip	/trɪp/
tropical	/ˈtrɒpɪkl/
trousers	/ˈtraʊzəz/
true (come true)	/truː/ /kʌm ˈtruː/
trunks (swimming trunks)	/trʌŋks/ /ˈswɪmɪŋ trʌŋks/
try	/traɪ/
try on	/traɪ ˈɒn/
tuberculosis	/tjuːbɜːkjʊˈləʊsɪs/
turtle	/ˈtɜːtl/
tutor	/ˈtʃuːtə(r)/
TV presenter	/tiː ˈviː prɪˌzentə(r)/
twin-bedded room	/twɪn bedɪd ˈruːm/
typical	/ˈtɪpɪkl/

U

ugly	/ˈʌglɪ/
Ugly Sister	/ˈʌglɪ ˈsɪstə(r)/
UK	/juː ˈkeɪ/
uncle	/ˈʌŋkl/
under	/ˈʌndə(r)/
under-18 nights	/ˈʌndə(r) eɪˈtiːn naɪts/
unfair	/ʌnˈfeə(r)/
unfortunately	/ʌnˈfɔːtʃənətlɪ/
unhappy	/ʌnˈhæpɪ/
United Kingdom	/juːnaɪtɪd ˈkɪŋdəm/
unlike	/ʌnˈlaɪk/
until	/ənˈtɪl/
unusual	/ʌnˈjuːʒʊəl/
up (up and down)	/ʌp/ /ʌp ən ˈdaʊn/
upset	/ʌpˈset/
upstairs	/ʌpˈsteəz/
USA	/juː es ˈeɪ/
use	/juːz/

V

valuable	/ˈvæljəbl/
van	/væn/
vast	/vɑːst/
version (rock opera version)	/ˈvɜːʒn/ /rɒk ˈɒpərə vɜːʒn/
very	/ˈverɪ/
vet	/vet/
video player	/ˈvɪdɪəʊ pleɪə(r)/
view (in our view)	/vjuː/ /ɪn ˈaʊə vjuː/
view (to have a good view of)	/vjuː/ /tə hæv ə gʊd ˈvjuː əv/
village	/ˈvɪlɪdʒ/
visit	/ˈvɪzɪt/
voluntary work	/ˈvɒləntrɪ wɜːk/
volunteer (n.)	/vɒlənˈtɪə(r)/
volunteer (v.)	/vɒlənˈtɪə(r)/

W

waist	/weɪst/
wait ▶ I can't wait!	/aɪ kɑːnt ˈweɪt/
wait for	/weɪt fə(r)/
Wales	/weɪlz/
walk all the way from ...	/wɔːk ɔːl ðə ˈweɪ frəm .../
wallet	/ˈwɒlɪt/
want	/wɒnt/
warm	/wɔːm/
was ◀ be	/wɒz, biː/

washing machine	/ˈwɒʃɪŋ məʃiːn/
washing up	/ˈwɒʃɪŋ ʌp/
(do the washing up)	/duː ðə wɒʃɪŋ ˈʌp/
watch	/wɒtʃ/
water	/ˈwɔːtə(r)/
waterfall	/ˈwɔːtəfɔːl/
way	/weɪ/
way (a long way from)	/weɪ/ /ə ˈlɒŋ weɪ frəm/
way (by the way)	/weɪ/ /baɪ ðə ˈweɪ/
way	/weɪ/
(She was on her way to ...)	/ʃiː wəz ɒn hɜː ˌweɪ tə .../
wear	/weə(r)/
web (the web)	/web/ /ðə ˈweb/
website	/ˈwebsaɪt/
weigh	/weɪ/
well	/wel/
well (as well as)	/wel/ /əz ˈwel əz/
well (as well)	/wel/ /əz ˈwel/
well (do well)	/wel/ /duː ˈwel/
Well done!	/wel ˈdʌn/
Well played!	/wel ˈpleɪd/
Welsh	/welʃ/
went ◀ go	/went, gəʊ/
were ◀ be	/wɜː(r), biː/
wet	/wet/
What sort of ...?	/ˈwɒt sɔːt əv.../
What would you like?	/wɒt wʊd juː ˈlaɪk/
wheelies (do wheelies)	/ˈwiːliːz/ /duː ˈwiːliːz/
while	/waɪl/
while (for a while)	/waɪl/ /fə(r) ə ˈwaɪl/
whistle	/ˈwɪsl/
whole	/həʊl/
wide screen TV	/waɪd skriːn tiːˈviː/
wife	/waɪf/
wild	/waɪld/
win	/wɪn/
winner	/ˈwɪnə(r)/
wish (make a wish)	/wɪʃ/ /meɪk ə ˈwɪʃ/
without	/wɪðˈaʊt/
wives	/waɪvz/
woke up ◀ wake up	/wəʊk ʌp, weɪk ʌp/
won ◀ win	/wʌn, wɪn/
wood	/wʊd/
wooden	/ˈwʊdn/
wool	/wʊl/
wore ◀ wear	/wɔː(r), weə(r)/
work	/wɜːk/
work out	/wɜːk ˈaʊt/
World Cup	/wɜːld ˈkʌp/
worn ◀ wear	/wɔːn, weə(r)/
worried	/ˈwʌrɪd/
worry ▶ Don't worry!	/dəʊnt ˈwʌrɪ/
Would you like (a cup of tea)?	/ˌwʊd juː laɪk ə kʌp əv ˈtiː/
Would you like (a dessert)?	/ˌwʊd juː laɪk ə dɪˈzɜːt/
wrap	/ræp/
wrist	/rɪst/
writer	/ˈraɪtə(r)/
written ◀ write	/ˈrɪtn, raɪt/
written down	/rɪtn ˈdaʊn/
wrong ▶ **What's he done wrong?**	/wɒts hiː dʌn ˈrɒŋ/
wrote ◀ write	/rəʊt, raɪt/

Y

yacht	/jɒt/
yard	/jɑːd/
Yes, please.	/jes, ˈpliːz/
Yes, that'll be fine.	/jes, ðætl bɪ ˈfaɪn/
Yes, that's fine.	/jes, ðæts ˈfaɪn/
yesterday	/ˈjestədeɪ/
yet	/jet/

Z

zebra crossing	/zebrə ˈkrɒsɪŋ/
zookeeper	/ˈzuːkiːpə(r)/

Macmillan Education
Between Towns Road, Oxford, OX4 3PP
A division of Macmillan Publishers Limited
Companies and representatives throughout the world.

ISBN 1405 01912 3

Designed by Mackerel Limited.
Illustrated by Mark Davis.
Cover design by Mackerel Limited.
Cover photo by Getty.

The authors and publishers would like to thank the following for permission to reproduce:

I Can See Clearly Now Words and Music by Johnny Nash copyright © Cayman Music Inc, Dovan Music Inc, Vanas Music Inc and Vanas Music, Netherlands, Warner/Chappell Artemis Music Ltd, London, W6 8BS 1986, reprinted by permission of International Music Publications Ltd. All Rights Reserved.

Love At First Sight Words and Music by Kylie Minogue, Richard Stannard, Julian Gallagher, Ashley Howes and Martin Harrington copyright © Mushroom Music International/The International Music Network Limited, Sony/ATV Music Publishing (UK) Limited and Biffco Music Publishing Limited/Universal Music Publishing Limited (20%) EMI Music Publishing Ltd, London, WC2H 0QY 2001, reprinted by permission of International Music Publications Ltd and Music Sales Limited. All Rights Reserved. International Copyright Secured.

Extracts from 'The teenagers' copyright © Telegraph Group Limited 1999 from 'Special Report T2' first published in The Daily Telegraph 13.11.99; 'School swap' copyright © Telegraph Group Limited 2000 from 'T2' first published in The Daily Telegraph 08.04.00 and 'Big city to beach' copyright © Telegraph Group Limited 2000 from 'T2' first published in The Daily Telegraph 26.02.00, all reprinted by permission of the publisher.

The publishers would like to thank the following for their help with the photographs; Kate Appleton, Aaron Baldwin, Yvonne Batty, Cherie Darbon, William Green, Martin Hibbert, Ben Jamieson, Felicity Lees, Robin Mackintosh, Luke Sabatini; Blackbird Leys Leisure Centre, Oxford; Cambridge City Council; The staff at Don Pasquale's Cafè, Cambridge; Sarah Meadows; Chris Wilcox and the staff of Oxford Brookes Sports Centre; Oxford Youth Hostel Association; Pizza Piazza, Oxford; Dr Robson and Partners Surgery, East Oxford; Scudamores Punting, Cambridge; Nick Smith; The Theatre – Chipping Norton.

Commissioned photography by Haddon Davies pp6, 10, 12/3, 14/5, 22(t), 23, 24, 32, 34, 36, 44, 46, 48/9, 56, 58/9, 60, 62, 68, 71, 80, 82, 84, 92, 94, 96, 108, 110, 116, 118, 120/1, 129.

Picture Research by Pippa McNee.

The publishers would like to thank the following for allowing us to reproduce their photographs;-
Alamy pp22(b), 88, 101(b); ©BBC Photo Library pp52/3; Anthony Blake Photo Library p124(t, Joff Lee)(b, David Marsden) 125(tl, Martin Brigdale)(tr, David Marsden)(bl, Joy Skipper)(br, Maximilian); ©Chris Bott p122; Bournemouth News and Pictures p112; Reproduced courtesy of Bloomsbury Publishing, Harry Potter and the Philosopher's Stone by JK Rowling (Bloomsbury) illustration by Thomas Taylor, Harry Potter and the Chamber of Secrets by JK Rowling (Bloomsbury) illustration by Cliff Wright, Harry Potter and the Prisoner of Azkaban by JK Rowling (Bloomsbury) illustration by Cliff Wright, Harry Potter and the Goblet of Fire by JK Rowling (Bloomsbury) illustration by Giles Greenfield p51; Corbis pp76(tl, Geray Sweeney), 76(br, Tom and Dee McCarthy), 77(tr, Buddy Mays), 77(bl, Robert Estall), 83(tl, Wolfgang Kaehler), 100(t, Richard Cummins), (b, Geray Sweeney), 101(t, Dewitt Jones), 104(Bryn Colton/Assignments Photographers), 119(Bettmann), 128(©Kelly/ Mooney), 130(tr, ©ER Productions), 131(b, Martyn Goddard); Fox Kids Cup p7, 8, 26(l); Philip Hollis/ The Daily Telegraph p16; Digital Vision p74; With thanks to El Hotelito Desconocido p89; Image Bank p130(tl); Kent News and Pictures p76(bc); Courtesy of The Northern Territory News p40; Photodisc p76(tr); Paul Bergen/Redferns Photo Library p134; With thanks to The Red Lion Hotel p87; Ronald Grant Cinema Archive pp 28(t, br), 106(Dreamworks/Universal Pictures, picture from Ronald Grant Archive); Stone pp77(tl, br), 130(b), 131(t); Taxi p76(bl); The Times pp26(r), 27; VPG Integrated Media, Inc. p64.

And a very special thank you to our Development Editor, Daniela Morini, and our Publisher, Emma Byrne, whose commitment and enthusiasm have contributed so much to this project.

Printed and bound in Spain by Edelvives
2009   2008   2007   2006   2005